# Working with Gemstones

# Working with
# Gemstones
## A Bench Jeweler's Guide

by Arthur Anton Skuratowicz & Julie Nash

**MJSA Press**
Professional Excellence in Jewelry Making & Design

*We dedicate this book to two totally different but equally important people in our lives—our Dads. Thank you both for all that you have taught us, all that you sacrificed for our education, and all that you continue to inspire us with.*

*There is Dad, the jeweler, who brought one of us into this business. You turned a child's melting of pennies in the back of the family jewelry store into a career that has gone places never imagined.*

*There is Dad, the cattle rancher, whom no one would ever believe is a literature buff. You've read this thing and corrected our spelling, our grammar, and all the sentences that just didn't make any sense.*

*So here's to you both for all the integrity you've brought to the both of us. Enjoy this one while you can, because the next thing we write will be for your wives.*

*Arthur Anton Skuratowicz*
*Julie Nash*

©2005 MJSA Press
ISBN 978-0-9713495-4-4
Library of Congress Control Number: 2005929483

All rights reserved. No part of this book may be reproduced in any form or by any electronic or mechanical means, including information storage and retrieval systems, without permission in writing from the copyright holders, except for brief passages quoted in review.

**Photo Credits**

**Arthur Skuratowicz**, AntonNash LLC, Colorado Springs, Colorado: All "Picture This" photos and pages 31, 37, 54, 86.
**Gary Dawson**, Goldworks, Eugene, Oregon: Cover and pages 2, 5, 6, 10, 15, 27, 31, 36, 41, 42, 46, 47, 51, 58, 59, 63, 67, 68, 72, 74, 79, 82, 87, 90, 92, 97, 101, 104, 109, 112, 114, 115.
**American Gem Trade Association (AGTA)**, Dallas: Cover and pages 16, 24, 28, 38, 44, 48, 52, 60, 64, 70, 76, 80, 82, 84, 88, 94, 98, 102, 106, 110.
**International Colored Gemstone Association (ICA)**, New York City: Pages 20, 56, 75, 93.

The majority of articles in this book originally appeared, in modified form, in *MJSA Journal* (formerly *AJM* Magazine), which is published monthly by Manufacturing Jewelers & Suppliers of America Inc. Subscriptions: U.S.: $47USD one year, $88USD two years; Canada and Central America: $60USD one year, $109USD two years; all other countries: $99USD surface/$141USD airmail one year, $177USD surface/$253USD airmail two years.

For information about subscribing to *MJSA Journal*, call 1-800-444-MJSA or 1-508-316-2132 (in U.S. and Canada only); e-mail *info@mjsa.org*; website *MJSA.org*.

Safety Notice: The contents of this book are solely the work of the authors and have not been tested or authorized by Manufacturing Jewelers & Suppliers of America, *MJSA Journal*, or MJSA Press. The use or application of information, practices, and/or techniques pertaining to jewelry manufacturing, jewelry repair, or other related topics in this book may be hazardous to persons and property, and they are undertaken at the reader's own risk.

Book design by Meg Castillo.

*Working with Gemstones: A Bench Jeweler's Guide* is published by MJSA Press, 8 Hayward St., Attleboro, MA 02703; 1-800-444-MJSA (U.S. and Canada only) or 1-508-316-2132; e-mail *info@mjsa.org*; website *MJSA.org*.

# Table of Contents

| | |
|---|---|
| 7 | How to Use This Book |
| 11 | Glossary |
| 16 | Alexandrite |
| 20 | Apatite |
| 24 | Aquamarine |
| 28 | Chalcedony |
| 32 | Diamond |
| 38 | Emerald |
| 43 | Extra Facets: Tool-Specific Dangers |
| 44 | Feldspar |
| 48 | Garnet |
| 52 | Jade |
| 56 | Lapis Lazuli |
| 60 | Morganite |
| 64 | Opal |
| 69 | Extra Facets: Metal Interactions With Stones |
| 70 | Pearl |
| 75 | Extra Facets: Organic Gems |
| 76 | Peridot |
| 80 | Quartz |
| 84 | Ruby |
| 88 | Sapphire |
| 93 | Extra Facets: Iolite |
| 94 | Spinel |
| 98 | Tanzanite |
| 102 | Topaz |
| 106 | Tourmaline |
| 110 | Turquoise |

**Gemstone Resources**

| | |
|---|---|
| 116 | Index to Resources |
| 117 | Diamond Council of America |
| 118 | GCAL (Gem Certification & Appraisal Lab) |
| 119 | GIA (Gemological Institute of America) |
| 120 | National Association of Jewelry Appraisers (NAJA) |
| 121 | Neutec/USA |
| 122 | Otto Frei |
| 123 | Rio Grande |
| 124 | About the Authors |

# How to Use This Book

This book attempts to offer some practical, "real world" advice for handling gemstones. There are already numerous publications expounding the beauty of gems, so we are focusing on how to keep those gems beautiful while cleaning them, setting them, and working around them. We have based our suggestions on the physical properties of the stones and our own experiences with handling them, as well as the experiences conveyed to us by other jewelers, manufacturers, appraisers, and gemologists.

We have divided the book into separate chapters for each

stone covered, and have also included a glossary of terms that are commonplace for a gemologist but may be unfamiliar to sales associates and a few bench jewelers. We've also included a few "extras." Among them, "Tool-Specific Dangers" presents an overview of common bench tools and their possible effects on gemstones, while "Metal Interactions With Stones" outlines alloy characteristics to help the jeweler choose the most appropriate metal for the job at hand.

Each gemstone chapter is divided into several categories:

**At a Glance:** This illustrated chart provides a quick, visual overview of each stone and its tolerance for torch retipping, torch sizing, pickling and plating, files and abrasives, polishing, and ultrasonic and steam cleaning. The key to the chart is below.

**Routinely done**
*Use caution*

**May cause harm**
*Extreme caution*

**Avoid if possible**
*Damage likely*

**Never**
*Total stone annihilation likely*

**Enhancements:** This section covers the main enhancements or treatments for each stone, and lists precautions.

**Clean It:** Cleaning jewelry seems so simple and worry free. However, many stones do not do well when subjected to standard cleaning procedures. In this section, we provide alternative cleaning methods and other cleaning do's and don'ts for each stone.

**At the Bench:** The meat of the book, this section details specific problems that can occur with each stone at the jeweler's bench. Some stones do not tolerate pickle solution, while others will explode if touched by a torch flame, or cleave or break with the slightest pressure. Read the whole section to avoid a critical caution that is specific to the stone with which you are working.

**Design It:** This section lists any special precautions needed when designing pieces featuring specific stones.

**Rock Solid Facts:** This section lists the hardness and type of fracture of the stone.

**Tools That Rule:** Here we note the (often obvious) tools that can make dealing with a particular stone easier for the bench jeweler.

**Bench Check:** Designed to act as a checklist for jewelers, this section asks questions that a jeweler should consider when working with a particular stone.

**Design Check:** Similar to Bench Check, this section asks questions that jewelers should consider when designing a piece featuring a particular stone.

**Features and Benefits:** After the serious business of preventing damage to stones, we thought it would be nice to highlight some of the positive aspects of each gem. This section gives you selling points for the gems discussed. It also provides you with tactful and positive segues for explaining a potentially hazardous setting or fragile stone.

**Picture This:** This photo gallery illustrates mostly bench and cleaning accidents—things you hopefully will not cause after reading this book.

**Care for Wear:** A critical part of the book, this section tries to protect you. Often customers assume that if an item is expensive, it is durable in proportion to its cost. With gems (even diamonds) this a bad assumption. Here we give tips for wear and care that, if passed along to customers, can save your business's reputation. (You should put specific care instructions in writing for each gem and make sure that a copy is given for each repair or sale of that stone.)

Of course, there will always be that inevitable instance when you take every precaution we have put forth, add a few of your own, and still end up with a broken stone. *It will happen!* The law of averages decrees this. So always protect yourself by having a written policy that details your responsibilities. Discuss this policy with clients when you take their items in for repair or setting, and have them sign the policy to signify their understanding and agreement. This may seem like overkill, especially during the take-in of inexpensive items. However, each time we have been involved in a situation in which a stone was damaged by a jeweler, everyone, including the customer, wished that there had been an iron-clad policy in place that spelled out how the situation would be handled.

Liability policies can vary and must fit your business and your personal ethics. Have your attorney review your policy to make sure that you are in compliance with state and local laws; you definitely want your policy to withstand legal scrutiny. You may also want to go beyond the letter of the law and offer your clients further protection, as a matter of maintaining a certain professional reputation in your community. One of our favorite stone damage policies says that, if stone damage occurs, the jeweler will replace it at no profit, i.e., the client pays the jeweler's cost for the stone (no markup). This may mean that a few jobs walk out your door, but in the long run you will come out ahead.

In the end, if you always use common sense when handling gems in your business or at the bench, you should have few problems. If in doubt, do not expose a gemstone to direct heat, temperature changes, chemicals, or physical trauma.

So go forth and conquer each gem—without chipping, scratching, cleaving, or other mishap.

# Glossary

**Abrasion:** A cluster of microscopic chips on a stone that appear as a dull area. It results from contact between a gemstone and an abrasive such as a file, sandpaper, or polishing compound. Abrasions usually occur on facet junctions or on the tops of stones.

**Adularescence:** A nebulous blue or white cloud that seems to float throughout moonstone.

**Alloy:** A mixture of metals. An alloy will have different properties and/or colors than the individual metals that compose it.

For example, the addition of copper to yellow gold will create a rose-colored gold, while adding nickel to yellow gold will create a white alloy. Sometimes these mixtures have mixed results: The addition of nickel, for example, makes gold not only white, but also brittle and hard—a potential headache for a stone setter. If you have questions concerning the properties of an alloy, contact its manufacturer.

**Bulge:** The description for a stone pavilion that is convex rather than straight, as it would be with a round brilliant-cut diamond. Bulges present difficulties in stone setting because more metal must be removed or moved to accommodate the stone in the mounting.

**Cat's eye:** A characteristic of some gemstones that produces the appearance of an elongated feline pupil. This effect is caused by light reflecting off of parallel needle-like inclusions within the stone. Chrysoberyl and tourmaline commonly have cat's eyes; such stones are considered "phenomenal" stones.

**Cleavage:** A property of minerals and gems that causes them to split in certain directions when subjected to sharp blows. Not all stones have cleavage, and those that do can split in more than one direction. Cleavage is important to the bench jeweler because extra care must be taken to avoid cleaving (splitting) stones with this property.

**Color change:** A characteristic exhibited by some gemstones in which the stone appears to be one color under fluorescent light and another color under incandescent light. Color change is described as a "phenomenon" and should not be confused with pleochroism or color zoning. Alexandrite is the most famous gemstone exhibiting color change.

**Color zoning:** A situation in which a gemstone exhibits two or more different colors in the same crystal. Color zoning results from the presence of color-causing impurities in different parts of the crystal. Some color zoning follows the crystal structure and some is random. An example of a color-zoned gem is watermelon tourmaline. Color zoning should not be confused with pleochroism or color change.

**Conchoidal:** A term describing a type of fracture that is shell shaped. This is the most common type of fracture or chip in gemstones.

**Cultured:** In regard to pearls, culturing is the process in which an irritant or bead is placed in a mollusk to initiate the formation of a pearl. In regard to gemstones, some synthetic gem manufacturers refer to their products as "cultured" instead of in terms such as "laboratory grown," "laboratory created," or "synthetic."

**Diffusion treatment:** A type of treatment where an undesirable or light-colored gemstone is heated in the presence of chemicals. The chemicals enter the surface of the gem, resulting in a layer of color that makes the stone more attractive. Diffusion treatment is most often done on sapphires and, less frequently, on ruby. Other stones are said to be diffusion treated, such as topaz, but this treatment may actually be a form of coating.

**Dispersion:** The rainbow (spectral) flashes of color caused by the refraction of light in a gemstone. Also known as "fire" in reference to diamonds.

**Enhancement:** Any process other than shaping that is done to a gemstone to improve or change the stone's appearance. Enhancements are the same as treatments. Heat, irradiation, dyeing, fracture filling, wax coating, laser drilling, and diffusion are all examples of enhancements.

**Feather:** A crack in a diamond, although occasionally the term will be used when referring to cracks in stones.

**Firecoat:** A solution of boric acid and alcohol used to keep oxygen off the surface of gemstones during torch work.

**Fracture filling:** A process in which a substance, usually an oil, polymer, or glass-like compound, is forced into surface-reaching cracks or fissures in a gemstone to make them less visible. The filling material will have similar optical properties to that of the gem, and in some cases dye may be added to intensify the body color. Emeralds in particular sometimes have dyes in their fracture fillings.

**Girdle:** The edge of the stone outline. The setting edge of a gemstone. Also known as the circumference edge.

**Granular:** The texture of a fracture that some gemstones exhibit. This texture is gritty or grainy in appearance and often resembles the surface of a sugar cube.

**Hardness:** A gem's resistance to scratching. Hardness should not be confused with toughness, which is a gem's resistance to breaking. A gem can be very hard but easily broken. In gemology, the Mohs scale is used to measure hardness.

**Heat treatment:** A process in which a gemstone is subjected to heat in order to change its color or clarity, or to induce phenomena, such as stars in corundum. Ruby, sapphire, tanzanite, aquamarine, and citrine are routinely heat treated to achieve familiar colors.

**Imitation:** Any natural or synthetic gem, as well as any other substance (glass, plastic, etc.), used to imitate another gem. For example, cubic zirconia is laboratory made and imitates diamond. Zircon is a natural stone that was often used to imitate diamond in the past. Glass rhinestones have also been used to imitate diamond.

**Irradiation treatment:** A process in which a gemstone is irradiated to change its color. Irradiated diamonds are usually bright yellow, green, or greenish blue, with other colors possible. Blue topaz is almost always the result of irradiation. Pearls can be irradiated to create a black color. Other gems can be subjected to irradiation treatment as well.

**Labradorescence:** A rainbow iridescence phenomenon found in labradorite.

**Laser drilling:** A process in which an opening (usually a narrow tube) is created in a diamond with a laser beam to introduce bleaching agents to dark inclusions. Recent innovations in laser drilling have resulted in drill holes that look like natural feathers or cracks in the diamond.

**Mohs scale:** A scale of hardness used for gems and minerals. The scale is comparative and not evenly spaced. For example, 10 is many times harder than nine, while eight is only somewhat harder than seven. The numbers are based on the hardness of the following minerals: talc (1), gypsum (2), calcite (3), fluorite (4), apatite (5), orthoclase feldspar (6), quartz (7), topaz (8), corundum (9), and diamond (10).

**Natural:** A gemstone mined from the earth. Some parts of the industry want to use the term "natural" to refer only to stones mined from the earth that have not been treated or enhanced. This viewpoint has not been widely accepted, so treated stones that come from the earth are usually referred to as natural. However, there are exceptions. For example, natural pearls are pearls that were not cultured by humans but were formed spontaneously by the mollusk.

**Oxidation:** A blackening or darkening of metal due to a surface reaction with oxygen. Oxidation can occur naturally over time or can be caused if certain chemicals are placed on the surface of the metal. The effect is often used on silver to highlight patterns in the metal, and it can also be used on karat gold. Black paint and similar substances, such as black ink or permanent marker, have been used to mimic oxidation.

**Parting:** A property of star rubies and sapphires in which the stones split in a manner similar to cleavage. There is no cleavage direction in these stones but rather a layering between multiple layers of growth within the gems.

**Pavilion:** The portion of a stone below the girdle.

**Phenomenal:** Optical characteristics of gemstones that include color change, play of color, cat's eye, star, adularescence, and labradorescence. These are visible and result from the interplay of light with the gem. Only a few gems are phenomenal, including opal (play of color), alexandrite (color change), chrysoberyl (cat's eye), labradorite (labradorescence), and moonstone (adularescence).

**Play of color:** An optical characteristic of phenomenal opal in which the refraction and interference of light produce an appearance of moving and changing color patches. Opals often have play of color.

**Pleochroism:** A characteristic in which colored gemstones exhibit different colors in different crystal directions. Not all colored stones exhibit pleochroism, or at least exhibit it strongly enough to be noticeable. Common strongly pleochroic gems include tanzanite (which shows blue in one direction and purple in another), andalusite (which is green and orange), and tourmaline (which can have a light and dark version of the same hue).

**Pressure point:** A raised or indented area of metal in the stone seat, or a raised or "lumpy" part of the stone's surface, that causes uneven force on the stone when metal prongs or bezel walls are pushed over the girdle. The uneven force can result in a chip or fracture of the gem. Pressure points on "lumpy" stones can be avoided if seats are burred to match the contours of the stone.

**Safety-edge file:** Any file that has the teeth ground off one edge and the resulting surface polished. This smooth, polished edge is the side of the file that should rest against the stone when shaping prongs.

**Seat:** The area cut out of a setting in which the stone sits. The seat should be cut to match the profile of the stone, an essential feature for any secure and durable stone setting.

**Star:** A characteristic of some gemstones, caused by the reflection of light off intersecting needle or tube inclusions, that produces the appearance of multiple rays on the surface of the stone. The number of rays in the star generally depends upon the type of gemstone. Corundum stars usually have six rays, while diopside stars have four. Gemstones with stars are considered "phenomenal" stones.

**Synthetic:** A gemstone made in a laboratory that has the same crystal structure and chemical formula as its natural counterpart.

**Table:** The large flat surface at the top of a faceted stone.

**Thermal shock:** The shattering of a crystal or other object due to sudden changes in temperature. Think of the crack heard when ice hits room-temperature water; that's the ice crystal suffering thermal shock. The same thing happens to gemstones, but with more severe economic consequences.

**Treatment:** Any process other than shaping that is done to a gemstone to improve or change its appearance. Treatments are the same as enhancements. Heat, irradiation, dyeing, fracture filling, laser drilling, wax coating, and diffusion are all examples of treatments.

**Waxy:** The luster of a fracture that some gemstones exhibit. The appearance is like that of candle wax and often makes the fracture easier to see due to the distinct luster difference.

# Gemstone Index

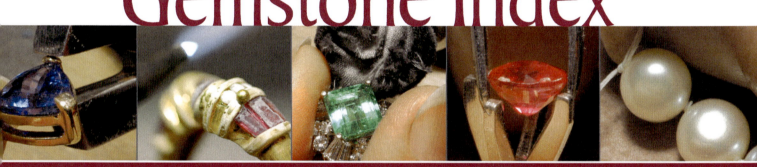

**Alexandrite** 16

**Apatite** 20

**Aquamarine** 24

**Chalcedony** 28
  Agate
  Bloodstone
  Carnelian
  Chrysocolla
  Chrysoprase
  Dendritic Agate
  Drusy
  Fire Agate
  Iris Agate
  Jasper
  Lace Agate
  Moss Agate
  Onyx
  Sard
  Sardonyx

**Diamond** 32

**Emerald** 38

**Feldspar** 44
  Amazonite
  Labradorite
  Moonstone
  Sunstone

**Garnet** 48
  Almandite
  Andradite
  Color Change
  Demantoid
  Grossularite
  Hessonite
  Malaia
  Pyrope
  Rhodolite
  Spessartite
  Tsavorite

**Iolite** 93

**Jade** 52
  Jadeite
  Nephrite

**Lapis Lazuli** 56

**Morganite** 60
  Bixbite
  Goshenite
  Heliodor
  Maxixe

**Opal** 64

**Organics** 75
  Amber
  Coral
  Shell

**Pearl** 70
  Cultured
  Natural

**Peridot** 76

**Quartz** 80
  Amethyst
  Ametrine
  Citrine

**Ruby** 84

**Sapphire** 88

**Spinel** 94

**Tanzanite** 98

**Topaz** 102

**Tourmaline** 106
  Chrome
  Paraíba
  Parti-colored
  Rubellite
  Watermelon

**Turquoise** 110

# Alexandrite

| Unique Hazards | Torch Retipping | Torch Sizing | Pickling & Plating | Files & Abrasives | Polishing | Steamer | Ultrasonic |
|---|---|---|---|---|---|---|---|
| High cost may dictate more careful handling than physical properties dictate | ⚠ | ⚠ | ok | ⚠ | ok | ok | ok |

Alexandrite is the color-change variety of the mineral chrysoberyl. One of the most valuable colored stones, alexandrite appears red to purple under incandescent (candle) light, and green under fluorescent light and daylight. The strength of the color change helps to determine the stone's value. Some stones tend to have weak color change that goes from a greenish gray to a reddish gray, as opposed to a very vibrant red to green change.

The traditional source for alexandrite is the Ural Mountains of Russia. Currently, the more prolific sources are Sri Lanka and Brazil.

## Enhancements and Imitations

Alexandrite is not known to be treated, but it is one of the most misidentified stones in jewelry today because of the various imitations and synthetics on the market. Synthetic alexandrite has the same chemical makeup and crystal structure as natural alexandrite, but it's made in a laboratory or factory. Prices for synthetic material are a fraction of those for comparable quality natural, but they vary depending on the method used in the material's manufacture.

Often available in sizes over 1 carat, synthetic alexandrite is very clear and exhibits a strong green/greenish blue to red color change. Microscopic examination by a competent gemologist offers the most reliable means of separating a natural from a synthetic alexandrite.

In our opinion, synthetic color-change sapphire is the stone most often misidentified as alexandrite. Synthetic color-change sapphires are generally worth only a few dollars. They are usually large and tend to have a blue to purple color change (occasionally the change is more greenish blue to purple). The huge value gap between natural alexandrite and synthetic sapphire makes it absolutely imperative for the jeweler to identify correctly any stone taken in for repair.

Another alexandrite pretender worth mentioning is andalusite, which does not exhibit color change, but has strong orange

## Quick Tips

### Rock Solid Facts
- Mohs Hardness: 8.5
- Cleavage/Fracture: Conchoidal

### Tools That Rule
- A safety-edge file to avoid abrading facet junctions when finishing prongs.

### Bench Check
- Have you had a gemologist verify that you are working with a natural alexandrite?

### Features and Benefits
- Alexandrite's color change makes it fascinating and unique.
- Alexandrite's durability makes it a good choice for everyday wear.
- Alexandrite is not known to be routinely treated—a huge selling point in today's treatment-laden jewelry trade.
- Alexandrite is recognized as one of the June birthstones.

## Picture This

> The same four stones pictured in fluorescent light on the left and incandescent light on the right. The marquise is a synthetic alexandrite, the oval is a natural alexandrite, the pear is a synthetic color-change sapphire, and the triangular cut is an andalusite. Note how the synthetic sapphire has a blue to purple change, while the alexandrites (synthetic and natural) change from green to purple. The andalusite shows little difference in color.

< Although alexandrite is very hard, the fluorescent light reflected off the table shows that the gemstone's surfaces can be scratched and abraded.

> This ring set with a synthetic alexandrite shows the typical color change from greenish blue (left) to purplish red (right) under different light sources.

and green pleochroism that causes it to be mistaken for alexandrite. Standard gemological tests will clearly separate imitations from natural alexandrite.

## Clean It

Alexandrite is very tough and very hard. Both steam and ultrasonic cleaning are considered safe. Other than andalusite, most stones mistaken for natural alexandrite can be cleaned by steam or ultrasonic.

## At the Bench

It is worth noting that the high value of alexandrite may influence how it is handled at the jeweler's bench. Despite its resilience, you may want to remove the stone from the setting if you are dealing with an especially large or strongly color-changing gem. Alexandrite is very hard to replace with exact color matches; therefore, many jewelers opt to treat it as they would a much more delicate stone.

Alexandrite is generally easy to work with at the jeweler's bench. Retipping should be avoided due to the expense of the stone, but sizing and other torch work can be done with an alexandrite in place. Also, pickling acids do not affect the stone. However, as with any colored stone, avoid thermal shock by letting a jewelry item air-cool prior to pickling.

When working with alexandrite, use a safety-edge file. Although it's one of the hardest gemstones, you can damage alexandrite by accidentally filing facet junctions while finishing prongs.

## Care for Wear

Alexandrite is very easy to wear. The hardness and toughness of the stone eliminate the need for special care. As with any colored gem, professional cleaning is recommended, as accumulated dirt gives the gemstone a dull appearance.

# Apatite

| Unique Hazards | Torch Retipping | Torch Sizing | Pickling & Plating | Files & Abrasives | Polishing | Steamer | Ultrasonic |
|---|---|---|---|---|---|---|---|
| Very soft, very brittle, and very sensitive to chemical etching | 💥 | ⚠️ | 💥 | 💥 | ⚠️ | ⚠️ | ⚠️ |

Although gaining in popularity, the colorful apatite has a delicate nature that will always limit its use in jewelry. It is usually found in bead jewelry, as well as the work of many fine art jewelers and craftspeople. This type of jewelry is often made through specialized techniques rather than the common processes used in commercial jewelry.

Most of the apatite seen in jewelry is a blue-green color similar to that of the more expensive Paraíba tourmaline. Lesser-known colors include yellow, purple, and pink. Colorless stones are also available. Apatite is found in India, Brazil, and Madagascar.

## Enhancements

Although there are no known enhancements for apatite, we believe that it is possible to fill the material with polymers, such as Opticon, to improve the durability of highly fractured pieces. We want to stress that this is our speculation based on our own experiments, and that we have not encountered this treatment.

## Clean It

Apatite is extremely sensitive to heat, so avoid steam cleaning unless you want a fractured stone. Ultrasonic cleaning can have the same unwanted result, especially if the solution is very hot. It is best to clean apatite with a soft brush and warm, soapy water.

## At the Bench

At the jeweler's bench, apatite requires a soft touch and lots of patience. With a five in Mohs hardness, this stone can be damaged by almost any jeweler's tool. To prevent this, avoid any contact with files, sandpaper, and polishing compounds. Even a soft buff charged with Tripoli or rouge can easily round facet junctions on an apatite.

The softness of apatite makes the stone highly susceptible to scratches and abrasions during setting and repair. The stone's two directions of cleavage make setting especially challenging because even a minimal amount of applied pressure can easily shear a stone.

Since apatite cannot tolerate heat, remove it from settings before performing any torch work. When removing it, use extreme care and move the metal in very small increments, since chipping can easily occur. If a stone cannot be removed, heat shields and water baths can be used, but caution still needs to be taken to avoid applying any heat to the stone. The best advice is to plan your torch work so that it can be done very quickly, minimizing

## Quick Tips

### Rock Solid Facts
- Mohs Hardness: 5
- Cleavage/Fracture: Two cleavage directions

### Tools That Rule
- A safety-edge file to avoid scratching or abrading the stone when finishing prongs.
- A laser welder for repairs with the stone in place.
- A water bath or heat shield to protect the stone from heat when removal is not an option.

### Bench Check
- Have you avoided pickle and acid-based plating solutions, which can etch the surface of an apatite?
- Is as much of the metal polished as possible prior to setting the stone?
- Have you taken precautions before performing any torch work?

### Design Check
- Is the piece constructed in a way that easily allows cleaning with a brush?
- Can the apatite in your design be removed if a repair is necessary in the future?
- Does the mounting protect the apatite from most sharp blows?

### Features and Benefits
- Apatite is a convincing alternative to extremely expensive Paraíba tourmaline.
- Apatite has a beautiful, bright color at a relatively low price.

## Picture This

> These apatite stones show the typical colors that are reminiscent of Paraíba tourmaline.

< This apatite has not been set or handled. Polish lines and abrasions are clearly visible and reveal apatite's delicate nature.

heat transfer to the stone. Of course, access to a laser welder is a wonderful way to deal with apatite-set pieces, if possible.

Apatite can be etched by acid, so avoid pickle and acid-based plating solutions. We remember one particularly skilled jeweler who plated an apatite-set custom pendant during his first week of work at a retail store. He had thought he was dealing with aquamarine and was flabbergasted by the frosty mess that he pulled out of the plating solution. As always, you must know the identity of the stone with which you're working.

## Design It

When designing an apatite-set piece, try to use delicate prongs that can be easily bent over the stone to avoid any excessive pressure that may chip the apatite. If bezel setting, try to use metal that is malleable and can be pushed over the stone with a minimum of pressure.

In addition, keep in mind that apatite is not a good choice for a ring or bracelet, which would put the stone in harm's way on a daily basis. Explain to customers that pendants, earrings, and brooches are the best ways to wear apatite and design your own pieces with this in mind.

## Care for Wear

Due to its fragile nature, apatite is too soft to stand up to day-to-day wear. Advise customers to avoid sleeping in apatite-set earrings, since rough fabrics could cause a loss of polish over time. In addition, hair care products, especially professional products such as permanent lotions and hair dyes, are likely to cause harm. Caution should even be taken with seemingly innocuous hazards, such as handbag straps and seat belts, which could damage apatite-set brooches and pendants.

# Aquamarine

| Unique Hazards | Torch Retipping | Torch Sizing | Pickling & Plating | Files & Abrasives | Polishing | Steamer | Ultrasonic |
|---|---|---|---|---|---|---|---|
| None | | | | | | | |

Aquamarine is the light slightly greenish blue variety of the mineral beryl. Although not as widely known as other beryls, such as emerald, aquamarine holds a prominent place in the jewelry industry and is recognized as the March birthstone. Aquamarine's color ranges from very pale to a moderately saturated, slightly greenish blue. Predominantly green aquamarine is also available and is gaining popularity among collectors and clients looking for something different.

Most aquamarine is mined in South America, particularly Brazil. Other sources include Madagascar, Africa, and the United States.

## Enhancements

Aquamarine comes out of the ground with a yellowish overtone, which gives the stone a light green or sea foam color. The vast majority of aquamarine on the market has been heat treated to remove the yellow component, resulting in a predominantly blue stone. The treatment is not detectable, and it is considered stable.

## Clean It

Aquamarine commonly has liquid-filled inclusions. When heated, the liquid inclusions expand faster than the surrounding gemstone and can cause the stone to fracture. Therefore, ultrasonic and steam cleaning are not recommended. However, most jewelers routinely ultrasonic aquamarine with no ill effects. If you do opt to use the ultrasonic, make sure that the fluid is not so hot that you can't put your fingers into it comfortably. This is a simple way to ensure that the temperature of the cleaning fluid won't cause the sudden expansion of the liquid inclusions. If you choose to live very dangerously and steam clean an aquamarine, be certain that you are willing and able to replace the stone if it shatters.

The safest way to clean an aquamarine is with a brush and warm, soapy water. We often dip the brush in the ultrasonic cleaning solution and then use it on the gem.

## At the Bench

Irradiated blue topaz and synthetic light blue spinel can closely resemble aquamarine in color. Since aquamarine is more valuable and requires different handling than both blue topaz and synthetic spinel, you must verify the stone's identity before beginning any repair work. The best method of identifying any

## Quick Tips

### Rock Solid Facts
- Mohs Hardness: 7.5 to 8
- Cleavage/Fracture: Conchoidal

### Tools That Rule
- A safety-edge file to avoid scratching or abrading the stone when finishing prongs.
- A water bath or heat shield to protect the stone from a jeweler's torch during sizing.
- Room-temperature pickle to avoid thermal shock.

### Bench Check
- Have you verified the stone's identity?
- Have you cut the seats in your aquamarine-set piece in a way that will not cause pressure points and stone breakage?
- Is as much metal as possible polished prior to setting the stone?
- If retipping, have you removed the stone?

### Design Check
- Have you designed a setting that allows the back of the stone to be easily cleaned?

### Features and Benefits
- Aquamarine is often cut into unique shapes that appeal to many tastes.
- Aquamarine is recognized as the March birthstone.

## Picture This

> The eye-visible scratches on this unfortunate aquamarine were the result of careless use of a sanding stick. Damage like this is difficult to justify to a customer.

< This aquamarine suffered extensive damage during prong setting. The large chip was the result of too much pressure being applied.

gemstone is to have a gemologist measure its refractive index.

Like most beryls, aquamarine cannot tolerate heat, and it must be removed from settings before you retip or do other torch work close to the stone. Sizings can usually be accomplished by placing the gem and its mounting in a water bath (Figure 1) or covering it with a heat-shielding product. You also must not quench an aquamarine-set piece in very hot pickle, as the sudden temperature change can cause liquid inclusions to expand and crack the stone. If you must pickle, use a room-temperature solution to avoid this potential problem.

Since aquamarine is often cut into custom or unique shapes, the setting's seats must match the outline of the stone. Any rough or raised areas in a seat can cause a pressure point that could lead to stone breakage. Pre-polish as much of the metal as possible prior to stone setting.

Although aquamarine is relatively hard, you must still exercise caution when using files and abrasives to finish prongs. A safety-edge file is highly recommended for shaping prongs with the stone in place. Avoid diamond- or corundum-based abrasives, since they will scratch aquamarine.

## Care for Wear

Aquamarine requires minimal special care from the wearer. However, the owner should be aware that aquamarine worn daily in a ring will probably require repolishing in a few years.

As with most light-colored gems, the accumulation of soap scum and lotion on the underside of the stone can greatly decrease its beauty. Therefore, you should recommend that the owner schedule regular cleanings.

# Chalcedony

| Unique Hazards | Torch Retipping | Torch Sizing | Pickling & Plating | Files & Abrasives | Polishing | Steamer | Ultrasonic |
|---|---|---|---|---|---|---|---|
| Dye may fade with prolonged exposure to light or heat (sunny windows) | 💥 | ⚠️ | ⚠️ | ⚠️ | ⚠️ | 💥 | 💥 |

Chalcedony encompasses the stones commonly known as agate or jasper. Technically, chalcedony is a cryptocrystalline form of quartz. In plain speak, this means chalcedony is an aggregate or tightly packed group of quartz crystals that are too small to be seen, even under a microscope.

Most of the chalcedony that we encounter is banded (striped) agate, opaque jasper, and dyed black chalcedony, which is referred to in the trade as black onyx. We could list hundreds of types of chalcedony with unique patterns and sources, and they can be found in almost any part of the world. Many agates are named for their places of origin or for the unique patterns they display.

The following are some of the more popular types of chalcedony.

**Agate:** A generic term for banded (striped) chalcedony. Usually named for its source, agate is found worldwide. Brazil is a large producer, with mines throughout the country.

**Bloodstone:** An opaque green chalcedony with red spots that can resemble blood droplets.

**Carnelian:** Orange to brownish orange chalcedony.

**Chrysocolla:** Bright greenish blue chalcedony colored by copper. Commonly found in the American Southwest, it is often mistaken for turquoise. Chrysocolla is one of the more expensive varieties of chalcedony.

**Chrysoprase:** Apple-green chalcedony colored by nickel. It can be found in Australia and is often mistaken for apple-green jadeite.

**Dendritic Agate:** Chalcedony with tree-like dendritic inclusions.

**Drusy:** Chalcedony with a coating of fine but eye-visible quartz crystals.

**Fire Agate:** Iridescent chalcedony found in Arizona.

**Iris Agate:** Chalcedony that shows interference colors in transmitted light. The colors have a rainbow appearance.

**Jasper:** Opaque chalcedony found worldwide and named for its source or pattern. "Picture jasper" is a popular type of jasper that has earth-tone patterns resembling landscape paintings.

**Lace Agate:** Chalcedony with a lace-like pattern of banding.

**Moss Agate:** Chalcedony with inclusions resembling green moss.

**Onyx:** Banded black-and-white chalcedony.

**Sard:** Brown chalcedony.

**Sardonyx:** Banded brown-and-white chalcedony. Often used to carve cameos.

## Quick Tips

### Rock Solid Facts
- Mohs Hardness: 6.5 to 7
- Cleavage/Fracture: Conchoidal or waxy

### Tools That Rule
- A laser welder to avoid having to remove a stone during repair.

### Bench Check
- Do you have a plan to avoid stone breakage during setting?
- Is as much metal as possible polished prior to setting the stone?
- Have you cut the seats in your chalcedony-set piece in a way that will not cause pressure points and stone breakage?

### Design Check
- Is your design one that will allow easy removal of the stone if necessary in the future?
- Does the piece allow for the back of the stone to be easily cleaned?

### Features and Benefits
- Chalcedony has a pattern for nearly any taste.
- Chalcedony fits any budget.
- Chalcedony lends itself to one-of-a-kind artistic carvings that appeal to those looking for uniqueness.

## Enhancements

Chalcedony may be enhanced by dyeing or heating. Heat treatment is usually performed on dull-gray specimens to turn them into more attractive and marketable orange/carnelian colors. It can be done in a standard kitchen oven and is thus widespread—and undetectable. If you have an orange chalcedony, assume it has been heat treated.

Because it is somewhat porous, chalcedony is very susceptible to dyeing. In fact, most black chalcedony (black onyx) is produced by dyeing a grayish or light-colored chalcedony. The stone can also be dyed emerald green, bright blue, purple, pink, and bright yellow. These colors are very bright, appear unnatural, and, if left in direct sunlight, may fade over time.

Due to the variety of colors possible through dyeing, some types of chalcedony can be misidentified. For example, dyed emerald green chalcedony in vintage pieces can be mistaken for emerald melée when in small sizes. Standard gemological testing using crossed polarized filters will differentiate the two. Also, while dyed blue jasper may look like lapis, it lacks the pyrite inclusions of that gem and tends to take a higher polish.

## Clean It

Due to the wide variety of chalcedony on the market, and the resulting range of durability, steam and ultrasonic cleaning are not recommended. While one type of agate may not break easily, another may tend to break on the boundaries, separating one color from another. Cleaning is best done with warm, soapy water. Also, avoid sudden temperature changes, which can cause chalcedony to shatter.

As with turquoise, chalcedony is often set in silver mountings. These mountings can have oxidized patterns (Figure 1, left). In many cases, the "oxidation" is merely black paint or a similar substance that can be removed easily during the cleaning process (Figure 1, right). To avoid altering the jewelry piece, check the item under magnification to verify if the oxidation is true chemical blackening before you clean it.

## At the Bench

Chalcedony cannot tolerate high temperatures. Torch heat on a chalcedony almost guarantees breakage. The prevalence of sterling silver settings exacerbates this situation; silver conducts heat very effectively and makes the use of water baths or heat shields risky. Therefore, chalcedony should be removed from the setting prior to any repair work requiring a torch. You can avoid this step by using a laser welder.

Torch heat isn't the only type of heat you need to worry about at the bench. We have personal experience breaking chalcedony while polishing, due to the friction produced on the silver setting. When working with chalcedony, polish carefully and try to pre-polish as much as possible before stone setting (Figure 2).

Also remember that metal polishing compounds and drusy don't mix. Once compound becomes stuck in the crystals, it may not come out without damaging the crystal layer. In fact, polishing abrasives in general pose problems with chalcedony-set jewelry. Files will leave noticeable damage on chalcedony, as will sandpaper and many of the rotary abrasives available for flex-shafts. The best way to avoid damaging the stone is good hand-eye coordination and tool control.

When setting chalcedony, you should take the utmost care to avoid breakage, since even slight pressure can chip a stone. Drusy chalcedony in particular requires extreme care; if the fine crystal layer is damaged, it can't be repaired. Many well-known gem carvers like to use chalcedony, and their pieces can be time-consuming to repair and expensive to replace, if replacement is even an option (thanks to the uniqueness of their carvings). Due to the unusual shapes and the particularly delicate nature of carved pieces and drusy chalcedony, seats must be cut very precisely. Doing so will lessen the potential for chipping the stone when you apply pressure to the metal during setting.

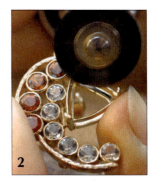

## Design It

The design of a chalcedony-set piece should allow for cleaning with gentle methods. Though they can be worn in rings, expensive types of chalcedony, such as chrysocolla, should be placed in settings that protect the stones from sharp blows. Drusy pieces and one-of-a-kind carvings should be set in pendants or brooches, as they will not survive the scrapes and blows of regular wear on bracelets or rings.

## Care for Wear

Heavy daily wear is not recommended for chalcedony. In particular, your customers should protect one-of-a-kind carvings and drusy from seemingly innocuous daily hazards, such as seat belts and handbag straps, since repair or replacement may not be possible.

## Picture This

> This chipped jasper shows the dull luster characteristic of chalcedony fractures.

< This drusy chrysocolla has a crystal-covered surface that is easily damaged by sharp blows or pressure from tools.

# Diamond

| Unique Hazards | Torch Retipping | Torch Sizing | Pickling & Plating | Files & Abrasives | Polishing | Steamer | Ultrasonic |
|---|---|---|---|---|---|---|---|
| None | | | | | | | |

Unarguably the most important gem in the industry, diamond isn't just another gemstone. Diamond has characteristics, such as hardness and thermal conductivity, that make it a major player in our technologically advanced world.

Hardness is one of diamond's best-known attributes. ("Hardness," in the gemological sense, is a gemstone's resistance to scratching.) This hardness—a 10 on the Mohs scale—makes diamond a very important industrial abrasive, and also allows it to be polished to a higher luster than many other gemstones, thus adding to its legendary appeal.

Prior to the discovery of diamonds in South Africa in the late 1800s, diamonds were generally owned by the super wealthy. During this time, diamond sources were limited to India and Brazil. India, in particular, has produced some of the world's largest and most famous diamonds, among which are the Idol's Eye, the Kohinoor, and the Hope. When Indian production began to decline, focus shifted to Brazil. When the Brazilian diamond fields were eventually depleted, South African sources filled the void and brought diamonds to the masses due to high production. (The African diamond fields ultimately gave rise to DeBeers and provided the African continent with one of its few true industries.)

In addition to Africa, diamonds are currently mined in Russia, Australia, and Canada. Australia's Argyle mine makes that country the world's largest producer by volume. However, that Australian mine is said to be slowing production as the source nears the end of its reserves. Canada is the latest arrival on the diamond scene. The stones mined in that country's Northwest Territories are high quality and, like the diamonds mined in Russia and Australia, can claim a "clean bill of health," in that they are not used to finance politically motivated wars, as are some diamonds of African origin.

## Enhancements

Diamonds can be enhanced in several different ways. In our opinion, you absolutely must disclose any and all such enhancements to potential consumers. But it is not enough to simply say "This diamond is enhanced"; you must enable the consumer to understand how it was enhanced as thoroughly as you do. This approach may seem like an attempt to kill the romance of a sale. However, because diamonds are purchased more than any other gem to commemorate milestones in life, full disclosure is imperative. As appraisers, we can tell you from experience that if anyone buys a fracture-filled stone as "clarity enhanced" without fully understanding that there is a substance other than diamond in their engagement ring, that person will never look at the purchase—or the jeweler—kindly again. On the other hand, a consumer who fully understands the treatment and still purchases the diamond doesn't have any reason for bad feelings.

**Irradiation** is one of the more established ways to treat a diamond. Diamonds of low or undesirable color are subjected to irradiation, followed by controlled heating, to achieve bright yellows, blue greens, greenish blues, and very dark greens. Red and pink diamonds occasionally result from radiation treatment as well. If done appropriately, the treatment emits no harmful residual radiation. (While the first attempts at radiation treatment involved radium salts, resulting in olive green diamonds that were highly radioactive, modern treatment carries no such risk.) If in doubt about the origin of a diamond's color, send it to a laboratory for advanced testing. Spectroscopic analysis can often identify a treated diamond.

**Coating the surface of a diamond** to change its color has been done for the last two hundred to three hundred years. The first incarnation of this treatment can be seen in antique jewelry, in which colored or silver foil was attached to the back of the stone. This would improve either the color of the diamond or the brilliance of the cut. However, these antique pieces usually have closed-back mountings, and any removal of the foil will hurt the jewelry's value. If you take in one of these items for repair, do not put it in an ultrasonic or steam cleaner.

Modern variations on coatings can range from nail polish or ink marker on the stone's girdle, producing the appearance of a

---

## Quick Tips

### Rock Solid Facts
- Mohs Hardness: 10
- Cleavage/Fracture: Step-like

### Tools That Rule
- A safety-edge file to avoid scratching or abrading the stone when finishing prongs.
- A laser welder to avoid burning platinum-set diamonds.
- Firecoat to avoid burning diamonds during torch work.

### Bench Check
- Have you checked the diamond for fracture filling in order to avoid heating a treated stone?
- Have you examined the stone for feathers near the setting edge and for thin girdle edges?
- Have you inspected the diamond for a coating that could be damaged or removed during bench work?

### Features and Benefits
- Diamonds match anything.
- Diamonds can be worn daily without worry.
- Diamonds represent special achievements and occasions.
- Diamond is recognized as the April birthstone.

fancy color, to high-tech thin films similar to those used on camera lenses. Because these treatments are unstable and can be easily removed, they are considered deceptive. If dealing with a fancy-colored diamond, examine the diamond to make sure no such treatment exists. (When examining it, look for iridescence on the surface or a "peeled paint" texture. Also, be suspicious of colors that appear too bright.) In any type of bench work except with a laser, the coating will probably come off, the color will alter significantly, and the customer will blame you for "ruining" the diamond. Luckily, coatings on modern pieces of diamond jewelry are quite rare.

**HPHT** is the high pressure/high temperature treatment of a diamond to improve its color. This treatment appears to be permanent and will hold up to cleaning and routine bench work. It is also very difficult to detect, although only a certain type of diamond (Type IIA) accepts the HPHT treatment and the majority of diamonds are not of this type.

Definitive identification of an HPHT diamond needs to be done through advanced testing by a laboratory. Reputable HPHT dealers laser-inscribe the girdle edge of the stone to disclose the treatment. However, these inscriptions can be polished off or inadvertently covered by mountings. Observation of HPHT diamonds in crossed polarized filters sometimes reveals characteristic strain patterns, but researchers are not convinced that these patterns are reliable. Gemologists have also noted that while HPHT- treated stones appear as though they should be very strongly fluorescent in daylight, they show no reaction when exposed to ultraviolet. If you suspect an HPHT-treated diamond and cannot find a laser inscription, send it to a laboratory for advanced testing.

**Laser drilling** is done to improve the apparent clarity of the stone. In this process, a laser is used on the diamond to form a tiny hole that leads to a dark inclusion. Introducing air in this way may be enough to mask the inclusion. If not, bleaching agents can be inserted to lessen its appearance. Laser drill holes are visible with microscopic examination.

A recent variation on traditional laser drilling uses the laser to cause a fracture that extends from the inclusion to the surface of the stone. The resulting opening, like the traditional laser drill hole, is used to introduce a bleaching agent. This type of laser drilling is very difficult to detect, since it is designed to appear as a surface-reaching feather. Both types of laser drilling are stable when subjected to routine cleaning and bench work.

**Fracture filling** is a treatment in which a glass-like substance fills a surface-reaching inclusion to mask its appearance. It can be achieved only when inclusions reach the surface of the diamond; if they don't, then laser-drill holes can be used as conduits for the filling material. Several companies perform this treatment, and their exact methods are proprietary. Fracture filling is often called "clarity enhancement," although it can also be referred to by the name of the company performing the treatment. Yehuda and Oved are two such eponymous names for these treatments.

Fracture filling can usually be detected with microscopic examination. The filling materials give colored flash effects in certain microscopic lighting conditions. Detection of this treatment is very important, as it is not considered completely stable to all forms of bench work. Cleaning is usually safe, but torch work can cause the filling material to seep out or become hazy. Manufacturers of fillers are improving their product, though, and recent fillers are said to be immune to torch heat. However, because it is impossible to tell the formula of the filling material, do not subject fracture-filled diamonds to direct torch work. If the filling is damaged at the bench, the stone can be repaired by one of the filling manufacturers.

## Synthetic Diamonds

Diamonds have been synthesized (made in a laboratory) since the 1950s. The vast majority of these stones are used as industrial abrasives. In more recent years, gem-quality synthetic diamonds have been produced, but they are not overly common in the jewelry trade. However, if you haven't yet seen synthetic diamonds in your daily business, the chances of your seeing them increase every day as production rises and more companies try to synthesize them.

Synthetic diamonds are produced using several methods, and a trained gemologist who makes a concerted effort to stay current on the latest developments can usually identify them. As you would with treated diamonds, be sure to inform the customer that a diamond is synthetic before beginning any work on an item. Failure to disclose the identity of a synthetic diamond could potentially be a nightmare for a jeweler, and you must know how to identify the stones as synthetic or have access to someone who can. Some things to look for when identifying a synthetic are very bright colors and odd-looking inclusions.

Synthetic diamonds can be treated as you would treat a natural diamond at the bench. If you are selling synthetics, check with the manufacturer to see if there are any recommended precautions. Changes in synthetics seem to come about every few years, and you must know the latest developments.

## Clean It

Most diamonds can be routinely cleaned by ultrasonic or steam. Exceptions include foil-backed antique pieces that would be ruined by any cleaning except that done with distilled water and a soft paintbrush. When cleaning these antiques, make sure that no moisture reaches the foil backings. Some jewelers also prefer to avoid ultrasonic and steam when cleaning fracture-filled diamonds. This is probably not necessary, but you should not leave fracture-filled diamonds in the ultrasonic cleaner all day, as is often done with diamond jewelry.

## At the Bench

Diamonds are known for being fairly foolproof at the jeweler's bench. Diamond tolerates heat well, as long as the stone is covered with firecoat (Figure 1). However, if a diamond is not covered with firecoat, the surface can burn during torch work and leave a white, hazy appearance on the diamond. Firecoat can also be burned off if torch work takes too long. Either way, the result will be a burned surface that effectively kills the sparkle of the stone and can be repaired only by re-polishing.

When working with platinum, you must use white gold solder for retipping with a torch, since firecoat won't protect a diamond from burning at the temperatures necessary to flow platinum solders (approximately 1,300°C/ 2,372°F, depending on the solder grade). We strongly recommend using a laser welder or sending platinum pieces out for laser welding (Figure 2) instead of mucking them up with white gold solder. This is especially true for vintage Edwardian and Art Deco diamond pieces from the early part of the 20th century, since white gold solder on vintage platinum pieces lowers their value.

What often causes trouble at the jeweler's bench is diamond's famous hardness. As jewelers, we can lull ourselves into thinking that a diamond can't be harmed, and we become careless. Although diamond is very hard and thus reasonably difficult to scratch, you should still use a safety-edge file when finishing prongs: Catching the teeth of a file on a facet junction can cause abrasion. This may not seem like a huge problem, but an abrasion could conceivably drop the clarity grade of a VVS1 diamond to a VVS2 or lower. When the clarity grade

---

## Picture This

> This is a top and side view of a diamond that was chipped in an attempt to tighten a prong. In the top view, note that the actual chip is on the upper left and that a reflection of the chip is visible as a white area on the lower right. The photo on the right shows the depth of the chip.

< Four laser-drilled holes and their reflections (at the bottom of the photo) are visible. Also note the pink and blue flash of fracture filling to the upper right. The presence of filling in a fracture leads to the conclusion that there is also filling in the drill holes. This diamond could easily be damaged if a torch is used on its surface.

> This diamond is shown before (left) and after (right) being subjected to the direct flame from a torch for approximately 10 seconds. If firecoat had been used to coat the stone, the milky surface burn would not have occurred.

drops, the value drops. We routinely look for this type of damage during appraisals.

Although diamond is hard, it has perfect cleavage—which means it can chip easily. Chipping usually occurs on corners or on thin, elongated cuts, such as baguette or marquise. Thin girdle edges also pose problems. To prevent chipping, carefully inspect the stone under magnification. Look for very thin edges and surface-reaching feathers near the edges of the diamond (Figure 3). If you can't avoid these potentially problematic stones, carefully cut the seats of the setting to match the shape of the diamond. This will help to lessen the pressure necessary to push the metal over the stone.

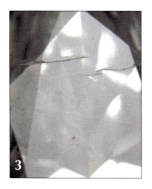

## Care for Wear

Diamonds require very little in the way of special care. However, we have all seen diamonds that have been chipped by customers. Common sense is the rule of thumb. Explain to customers that wearing their diamond jewelry during activities such as rock climbing and tennis is not advisable. However, there are also those strange instances when a diamond is chipped but the culprit can't be identified. Mystery chips happen, and their potential occurrence should be discussed with the owner's insurance carrier when policies are obtained.

The other issue with diamonds and daily wear is keeping the stones clean. Dirty diamonds don't sparkle, so regularly scheduled professional cleanings are a good idea. This also allows you, as the jeweler, to check stones for security and prong wear, as well as repair any potential problems before stones are lost.

▶ The abrasions on the facets of this diamond are the result of daily wear and a jeweler's file during prong finishing. Although hard, diamonds can still be damaged by careless filing practices.

◀ These three diamonds are fracture filled. The top view shows gas bubbles trapped in the filling material. However, if the stone was set or if magnification was not used, the filling could easily be overlooked. The side views on the bottom show the typical colored flash effect of the filling material. It is important to look at a diamond in several positions so as not to overlook any fillings.

▶ The corner of this triangular diamond was chipped when too much pressure was applied during setting.

# Emerald

| Unique Hazards | Torch Retipping | Torch Sizing | Pickling & Plating | Files & Abrasives | Polishing | Steamer | Ultrasonic |
|---|---|---|---|---|---|---|---|
| None | 💥 | ⚠️ | ⚠️ | ⚠️ | ⚠️ | ⚠️ | 💥 |

Its popularity dating back thousands of years, emerald is the most prominent member of the beryl family, which includes aquamarine, morganite (pink beryl), and heliodor (golden beryl). The rich, vibrant green of the emerald is caused by trace amounts of chromium in the crystal. Vanadium can also cause the green color, but the international gemological community disagrees on whether a vanadium-colored beryl is actually an emerald.

The very existence of a quality emerald ranks as a small miracle, since chromium does not easily insert itself into the beryl crystal. Thus, there are few viable sources for emeralds.

Colombia is the most famous source of quality emerald, which can also be found in Brazil, Zambia, Pakistan, and Afghanistan.

## Enhancements

Emeralds commonly feature fractures, and these fractures are routinely filled—with oils in antiquity, and oils or polymers in the present. However, since fracture filling has been done for as long as anyone can remember, it has not been generally disclosed to the consumer. In recent years, this has created a media furor and blatant misunderstanding. In this day and age of disclosure, fracture filling can be viewed as deceptive when pointed out by anyone other than the original seller. Therefore, disclose the presence of fracture filling in any emerald you sell unless you have laboratory documentation indicating lack of treatment. It is also important, as with many other gem treatments, that customers understand clearly that a particular stone would likely lack any appeal without being fracture filled.

Before working on emerald-set jewelry, you must take into account the filling material. Unfortunately, it is often difficult, if not impossible, to identify the exact substance used. Some in the emerald trade prefer oils because they are the traditionally accepted substance. But oil is unstable and can discolor over time or leak out of fractures, especially in the presence of detergents or heat. Others in the trade prefer polymers or other high-tech substances that have greater color stability and harden once they fill the fracture. However, unless you know the exact substance used in the treatment process, assume that it is oil and take appropriate precautions.

## Clean It

Cleaning an emerald needs to be approached with care. Ultrasonic cleaners are not recommended, since the detergent and heat can remove oil-based fracture-filling materials, causing the emerald to appear radically damaged. Fillers can be replaced, but showing a client his or her emerald after you have inadvertently cleaned out the filling material will not be one of your happier moments. There is some debate as to whether an ultrasonic can damage the actual stone and not just the filling material. We suggest that you not put any emerald in an ultrasonic cleaner, unless you are willing to replace it.

Steam cleaning can also damage emeralds. Many emeralds have large liquid-filled inclusions. The sudden temperature change caused by the steamer can make the liquid expand more

## Quick Tips

### Rock Solid Facts
- Mohs Hardness: 7 to 8
- Cleavage/Fracture: Conchoidal

### Tools That Rule
- A safety-edge file to avoid scratching or abrading the stone when finishing prongs.
- A laser welder to allow stones to be left in place during repairs.
- A water bath or heat shield to protect the stone from a jeweler's torch during sizing.
- A flex-shaft equipped with small polishing buffs and disks for a last-minute polish that won't damage the stone.
- A hydro-torch has a concentrated flame that can be directed to very specific areas, minimizing the chance of overheating the stone.

### Bench Check
- Are seats properly cut to avoid emerald breakage?
- Is as much metal as possible polished prior to setting the stone?
- Can the jewelry piece be finished prior to setting the emerald?

### Design Check
- Can the emerald in your design be easily removed if a repair is necessary in the future?
- Is the piece designed in a way that easily allows cleaning with a soft brush?
- Is the stone protected by the mounting from most sharp blows?
- Is the piece designed with thin prongs made of malleable metal to prevent stone breakage during setting?

### Features and Benefits
- Emerald is the classic green stone, which makes it a fashion must.
- Emerald is recognized as the May birthstone.

rapidly than the emerald surrounding it and crack the stone. Again, if you don't feel that you can replace the emerald, don't steam clean it.

The safest way to clean an emerald is with a soft brush and warm water. If you are unsure whether the emerald has been filled, the safest course of action is to assume that it has been and treat it accordingly.

## At the Bench

Emeralds present some special problems for the bench jeweler. The stone's softness makes it highly susceptible to scratches and abrasions during setting and repair. To avoid such damage, pre-finish and polish as much of the mounting as possible prior to setting the emerald. If you use a file, make sure that you create a safety edge by grinding the teeth off the edge of the file that will rest against the stone during finishing.

Metal polishing compounds can damage emeralds when the settings are polished with the stone in place. Also, the facet junctions of an emerald can be, and often are, accidentally rounded when buffed on a polishing machine. Sometimes this is noticeable only with magnification, but too often the damage is eye visible. An emerald with facets that have been rounded in this way loses some of its ability to reflect light and won't seem as sparkly as an undamaged stone. To avoid this problem, pre-polish as much of the setting as possible and, once the stone is set, use a flex-shaft to finish the polishing if necessary (Figure 1). The flex-shaft allows more control and offers a better chance of not hitting the stone with the polishing compounds.

Emerald's intolerance to heat makes using a torch near it inadvisable. The safest course of action is to remove an emerald from the setting before attempting any standard torch work. You can size a ring with the stone in place, but you must use a heat-shielding product or water bath to protect the emerald (Figure 2). A hydro-torch can be helpful because its small flame allows for precise control over where the heat is directed. Of course, access to a

## Picture This

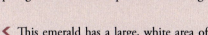
> This emerald was chipped during a tightening procedure. This was due in large part to gaps in the seat of the prong and/or excessive pressure in setting.

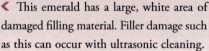
< This emerald has a large, white area of damaged filling material. Filler damage such as this can occur with ultrasonic cleaning.

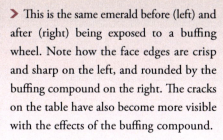
> This is the same emerald before (left) and after (right) being exposed to a buffing wheel. Note how the face edges are crisp and sharp on the left, and rounded by the buffing compound on the right. The cracks on the table have also become more visible with the effects of the buffing compound.

< This emerald was heated by indirect heat from a torch when the flame was deflected off of the metal. Surprisingly, the stone did not shatter, but it did become cloudy and dull. This particular stone highlights the risk of leaving an emerald in a setting while doing torch work—even away from the stone.

laser welder offers an ideal solution when dealing with repairs on emerald jewelry.

Remember that chemicals can often damage the filling material in an emerald. Thus, pickle solutions should be avoided. Again, if any work requires pickling, try to do it before the emerald is set or after it has been removed. To prevent accidentally pickling an emerald-set piece, keep your pickle pot covered.

## Design It

You should design a piece of jewelry so that it protects an emerald while minimizing the possibility of damage during setting. Use platinum or 18k yellow gold for prongs or bezels, since these metals tend to be easier to push over the stone than 14k yellow gold or 18k white gold. The less pressure needed to secure the stone, the less the chance of its breaking. To lessen the actual pressure needed for setting, use multiple thin prongs (Figure 3) as opposed to a few heavy prongs. If you do decide to use heavy prongs, make sure the stone setter anneals the metal, pre-bends the prongs, and cuts a very precise seat to make the setting process less stressful to the stone.

Emeralds tend to abrade with daily wear in a ring or bracelet. To lessen the abrasions that occur over time, design a ring in which a metal element is raised above the stone. Pay particular attention to which hand or arm the ring or bracelet will be worn on and whether the wearer is right- or left-handed.

## Care for Wear

Since rings are subjected to frequent stress, an emerald in a ring worn every day will become abraded. If wearing an emerald ring only on special occasions is unacceptable to the wearer, he or she should expect to re-polish the stone at some point, if not replace it outright. To prolong the life and beauty of an emerald ring, it should not be worn during activities that involve strenuous use of the hands, such as lifting weights, gardening, or golfing. You can also suggest to clients not to wash dishes or to wash or lotion their hands while wearing an emerald ring. Just as ultrasonic and steam cleaning pose dangers to the stone, cleaning soap scum or lotion off an emerald ring can prove difficult.

Earrings, necklaces, and pins are not usually subjected to the stress that rings are. However, to keep stones looking their best, soaps, shampoos, and conditioners should be avoided. In other words, customers shouldn't shower with their emeralds. Sleeping with emeralds on will also abrade the stones over time, since sheets are abrasive and can have the same effect on facets as metal polishing compounds.

## EXTRA FACETS
# Tool-Specific Dangers

Desirable jewelry is more than the sparkle of gems and the shine of metal. Rather, it's the perfect combination of these qualities: Metal and gemstone united to create a work of art. But to create this art, you must wield various tools to cut, shape, and finish your masterpiece. It is during this tool-use phase, otherwise known as manufacturing, that gemstones are at their most vulnerable. This section is an overview of common jewelry manufacturing tools, and their unique and specific hazards.

**Abrasive wheels/compounds:** To avoid scratching, abrading, and discoloring gemstones, check with the supplier for the specific content of the abrasives you are using. Diamond- and corundum-based compounds will damage most gemstones.

**Buffer/buffing compounds:** Friction heat from buffing may cause stone breakage. Buffing can also round facet junctions on soft stones. In addition, buffing compounds can discolor porous gems. Softer stones can easily be damaged by many of the compounds on the market. Check with the supplier for specific cautions.

**File:** When in contact with a gemstone, a file can cause scratches, chips, and abraded facet junctions. Use a safety-edge file to avoid damaging stones.

**Firecoat:** Used to keep oxygen off of the surfaces of gemstones during torch work, firecoat can become attached to the surface of corundum if pieces are overheated.

**Hammer:** Hitting a stone directly can cause chipping or shattering. The vibration from hammering on ring shanks or other parts of jewelry not directly touching a stone can be carried to the stone by the mounting and cause stone breakage.

**Hydroflux torch:** Offering greater heat control during torch work, a hydroflux torch has the benefit of having a flux in the flame that reduces the necessity for firecoat. If using a hydroflux torch, follow the manufacturer's instructions to make sure the flux is providing the expected protection to the stone.

**Laser welder:** While laser welders allow stones to remain in place during retipping, they may shatter stones if a beam hits the stone directly or by way of a ricochet.

**Pickle pot:** Hot pickle can cause stones to suffer thermal shock and shatter. The chemicals in pickle can also damage the surface of some gems (especially peridot and organics such as pearl), or damage treatments such as fracture fillings.

**Plating solutions:** Some gems (such as apatite, peridot, and pearls) are damaged by the chemicals found in most plating solutions. Even the less-toxic acid-based solutions may be harmful to acid-sensitive gems.

**Pliers:** Pressure from pliers applied to a gem during setting can cause chips or breakage. Pliers of any type need to be in good working order so that sudden pressure is not unintentionally applied due to sticky mechanisms or worn grasping surfaces.

**Sandpaper:** Can scratch and abrade gemstones.

**Steam cleaner:** Hot steam from a cleaner can cause thermal shock and shatter gems. Liquid inclusions in gems can expand with heat from the steamer and shatter the stone, particularly emerald, topaz, and tourmaline.

**Torch:** Direct heat from a torch will shatter most gems, and indirect heat can shatter many gems. The torch's heat can also be transferred to a gem by the mounting, again leading to damage. Torch heat may also discolor stones and melt fracture fillings.

**Tumbler:** If used to polish pieces with stones in place, tumblers may round the facets of some gems.

**Ultrasonic cleaner:** The hot solution in an ultrasonic can cause thermal shock and shatter gems. The chemical cleaning fluid can also damage fracture fillings (especially in emerald) or be absorbed into porous stones, such as turquoise or opal. In addition, the vibration from an ultrasonic can cause gems to shatter.

# Feldspar

| Unique Hazards | Torch Retipping | Torch Sizing | Pickling & Plating | Files & Abrasives | Polishing | Steamer | Ultrasonic |
|---|---|---|---|---|---|---|---|
| Avoid direct pressure | 💥 | ⚠️ | ⚠️ | ⚠️ | ⚠️ | 💥 | 💥 |

Several moderately well-known gems are varieties of feldspar. **Moonstone** is the most common, followed by **sunstone** (facing page) and **labradorite**. **Amazonite** is a lesser-known variety of feldspar that is often confused with turquoise because of its green-blue color.

This is an interesting group of gems in that many are "phenomenal." Moonstones exhibit adularescence, which is the nebulous blue or white cloud that seems to float throughout the stone. Labradorite has a phenomenon called labradorescence, a rainbow iridescence specific to that stone. Sunstone feldspar is not phenomenal in the gemological sense, but often has very interesting natural copper or hematite inclusions that give it a shimmering appearance.

Although feldspar can be found worldwide, the varieties used in jewelry are more limited in their sources: Labradorite is commonly found in Labrador, Canada, the region that gives the stone its name; moonstones are commonly found in the Indian subcontinent; and sunstone is found in Oregon and Sri Lanka.

## Enhancements

Feldspars are not commonly treated. Occasionally, amazonite may be irradiated to enhance its green-blue color, or it may be waxed to improve luster. The other gem feldspars are basically enhancement-free. Sometimes, moonstones may be backed with a black substance to improve the appearance of the stones' adularescence. These backings can range from spray paint applied directly to the back of the stone to black paper placed under a stone in a closed-back bezel.

## Clean It

Feldspars are not the most durable of gemstones, and therefore should be cleaned with the utmost care. Ultrasonic and steam cleaning are considered dangerous for these stones. The safest method is to use warm, soapy water and a soft brush. Although many jewelers have cleaned feldspar in an ultrasonic with no ill effects, you shouldn't take risks with a customer's stone.

As a side note, any moonstone that has been backed with a black substance is not likely to stand up to ultrasonic or steam cleaning; both methods will easily remove any backings, and the result will be obvious and likely unappealing to your customer.

## At the Bench

Cleavage is the most problematic aspect of working with feldspars. Because all gem feldspars have perfect and distinct cleavage, even a minimal amount of applied pressure can easily shear a stone. Since the gem feldspars are usually cut as cabochons and thus often bezel set, the probability of cleaving a stone through

# Quick Tips

### Rock Solid Facts
- Mohs Hardness: 6 to 6.5
- Cleavage/Fracture: One perfect cleavage and one distinct cleavage direction

### Tools That Rule
- A safety-edge file to avoid scratching or abrading the stone when finishing prongs.
- A water bath or heat-shielding product to protect the stone from the heat of a torch.
- A laser welder for repairs with the stone in place.
- A lid for the pickle pot to avoid accidentally pickling the stone.

### Bench Check
- Do the seats fit the profile of the stone as closely as possible?
- Have you avoided pickle, which can dull a stone's surface and damage backings?
- If retipping, have you removed the stone?

### Design Check
- Can the stone in your design be easily removed if a repair is necessary in the future?

### Features and Benefits
- Feldspars often have a phenomenon that appeals to the customer who really appreciates unique items.
- Most feldspar is affordable and can fit into any budget.
- The abundance of shapes, colors, phenomena, and quality appeal to any buyer.
- Moonstone is recognized as one of the June birthstones.

setting pressure is high. Extra attention must be paid to cutting the stone seat in the bezel properly (Figure 1). The seat should match the profile of the feldspar so that no areas of metal stick up and exert pressure on the stone when the bezel is pushed over. This is also true of prong setting.

With the exception of certain types of sunstone, most of the feldspars are not overly expensive. However, many times their unique appearance makes them difficult to replace. Labradorite in particular can vary widely in color and strength of phenomena. Moonstones are also often cut or carved into unique shapes; Edwardian-era jewelry often features carved moonstone cameos, which if broken are basically impossible to replace. Moonstones pose particular problems when one of a matching set must be replaced. You have to not only find the right body color of the moonstone, but also match the strength and shape of the adularescence (Figure 2).

In repair situations, keep in mind that feldspars cannot tolerate heat from a jeweler's torch. The safest course of action in performing a repair on a piece of feldspar-set jewelry is to remove the stone. If this is not feasible, use a heat-shielding product or water bath to protect the stone during torch work. Retipping with the stone in place is not possible unless done with a laser welder.

Pieces set with black-backed moonstones can be particularly problematic, since even the slightest heat can damage some backings. Water baths, which usually protect gems, can also damage some types of backings. Removing the stone is especially recommended in these instances.

Feldspars are particularly sensitive to being scratched at the bench; therefore, use a safety-edge file when finishing prongs and bezel settings (Figure 3). Avoid inadvertently hitting the stones with sandpaper or very aggressive polishing compounds, or damage may occur.

After soldering a feldspar-set piece, you should forgo pickling. The acids found in pickle and some plating solutions can dull a stone's surface to varying degrees, depending on the strength and type of acid, as well as the type of feldspar. Also, the black backing on many moonstones will not stand up to the pickling process. The safest route is to avoid any possibility of damage.

## Design It

When designing jewelry for feldspar items, be sure to engineer the piece in a way that allows it to be easily serviced in the future. Make sure that the stone is reasonably easy to remove from the setting for future repairs or stone replacements. For example, prong settings tend to make stone removal easier than bezel settings.

## Care for Wear

Cleavage is again the big issue with wearing feldspar. Because the stone cannot withstand heavy blows, active daily wear is not advisable. On the other hand, since many types of feldspars are relatively inexpensive, the option of replacing the stone in the event of damage can be explored with the client. However, when explaining this option, do not downplay the fact that it is sometimes difficult to match the exact color and strength of phenomena.

## Picture This

> This photo shows a close-up of fractured feldspar. The step-like structure of the chip is clearly visible.

< This photo shows the phenomena of labradorescence in a labradorite. The completely missing corner is the result of pressure applied in an attempt to set the stone, which broke easily.

> During the setting process, pay close attention to the internal fractures in this moonstone. Avoid applying excess pressure to these areas, which can break easily.

# Garnet

| Unique Hazards | Torch Retipping | Torch Sizing | Pickling & Plating | Files & Abrasives | Polishing | Steamer | Ultrasonic |
|---|---|---|---|---|---|---|---|
| None | 💥 | 🚫 | 🚫 | 🚫 | ✓ | 🚫 | ✓ |

The term garnet encompasses several well-known varieties that have a strong presence in the jewelry industry. Chemically, garnets can be quite different from one another. It is the chemical structure—the way in which the chemical components are combined—that defines a gemstone as a garnet. Jewelers can identify different types of garnets by visual observation of color and gemological testing.

Red is the color most often associated with garnets; however, green, orange, purple, yellow, and other colors are also common. The following page has a list of garnets with their descriptions.

**Almandite:** Orangey red to purplish red. Found worldwide, it's the most common type of garnet seen in jewelry. Almandite may come in dark orangey reds that appear brownish.

**Andradite:** Red, brown, yellow, green, or black calcium-iron garnets. Demantoid is the most valuable of the group.

**Color Change:** Garnets that show a change in body color when viewed under different light sources. Chemically related to malaia garnets, they are commonly found in East Africa.

**Demantoid:** Yellowish green with strong dispersion. Part of the andradite garnet group, demantoid is historically found in Russia and Italy, and it's commonly seen in Victorian jewelry. It is currently the only type of garnet known to accept heat treatment.

**Grossularite:** Pale green, pink, brown, or black calcium-aluminum garnets. Tsavorite is the most valuable of the group.

**Hessonite:** Yellow-orange to reddish orange and part of the grossularite group. It is commonly found in Africa, South America, and India.

**Malaia:** Pinkish orange to reddish orange and a chemical combination of the pyrope and spessartite groups. It is found in East Africa.

**Pyrope:** Reddish orange to dark red. Common in Victorian jewelry from central Europe, pyrope is found in the Czech Republic, South Africa, Australia, and the United States. It can closely resemble ruby in color.

**Rhodolite:** Reddish purple to purplish red. The more purely purple stones are known commercially as "raspberry" or "grape" garnet. Chemically a combination of almandite and pyrope, rhodolite is found in Africa, Sri Lanka, and the United States.

**Spessartite:** Yellowish orange to reddish orange, with bright orange gems often referred to as "mandarin." It is found in Brazil, Africa, Australia, Myanmar (formerly Burma), and India.

**Tsavorite:** Bright green to yellowish green and part of the grossularite group. It is found in the Tsavo Park region of Tanzania.

## Quick Tips

### Rock Solid Facts
- Mohs Hardness: 6.5 to 7.5
- Cleavage/Fracture: Conchoidal

### Tools That Rule
- A safety-edge file to prevent abrading the stone when finishing prongs.
- A laser welder to allow stones to be left in place during repairs.
- A water bath or heat shield to protect the stone from a jeweler's torch during sizing.
- Room-temperature pickle to prevent thermal shock to the stone.

### Bench Check
- Have you cut the seats for your garnet-set piece to match the outline of the stone?
- If retipping, have you removed the stone?

### Features and Benefits
- Garnets are available in a wide range of colors that appeal to nearly any taste.
- Garnets are available in many price ranges that fit most budgets.
- Garnets are durable and suitable for daily wear.
- Garnets are not known to be routinely treated.
- Garnet is recognized as the January birthstone.

## Picture This

> This was once a rather spectacular tsavorite garnet. When a jeweler heated the setting in which it sat, the unprotected stone completely shattered.

◄ This rhodolite garnet shows abrasions on the pavilion. The white lines visible through the table are the abraded facet junctions on the back of the stone, likely the result of jumbling the stone with others after cutting or during storage.

# Enhancements

The garnet group is rare in that there are no routine treatments to change color or clarity. The only known exception at this time is demantoid garnet from Russia, which can be subjected to low-temperature heat treatment to improve color.

# Clean It

Since garnets don't tolerate sudden temperature changes, don't steam clean them; opt for ultrasonic cleaning instead. However, ultrasonic cleaning of any garnet-set vintage pieces could lead to stones coming out of their settings. Most garnets are moderately priced and relatively easy to replace if a problem occurs due to cleaning. However, tsavorite and demantoid are quite expensive, with prices easily reaching $3,000 to $4,000 per carat in the wholesale market. Custom gem cutters especially favor rhodolite and other varieties, such as mandarin spessartite, and many of the specialized cuts are difficult to replace.

# At the Bench

Garnets are quite durable and present few problems for the bench jeweler. However, when working with garnets, you must always remember that they do not tolerate sudden extreme temperature changes; therefore, torch work cannot be done near or on the stone. Retipping or repairs on stone settings must be done after the garnet has been removed (Figure 1). Of course, if a laser welder is available, the garnet can be left in place. When sizing, place the garnet in a water bath or cover it with a heat-shielding product (Figure 2).

When pickling garnet-set jewelry, make sure the pickle is room temperature to avoid thermal shock to the stone. If you want to play it safe, allow pieces to air-cool prior to pickling, but this shouldn't be necessary if stones have been properly heat-shielded and the pickle is room temperature.

Since custom carvers favor garnet, the shapes of the stones are often unique. Thus, when stone setting, make sure the seats are cut neatly and cleanly, and that they match the shape of the stone. This prevents raised areas that cause "pressure points," which can result in stone breakage.

As with any gemstone, use a safety-edge file to finish prongs to avoid abrading or scratching the garnet.

# Care for Wear

Garnets require very little in the way of special care. If worn on a daily basis, a stone may become abraded over the course of several years and require re-polishing. As with any stone, professional cleaning on a regular basis is an easy way to maintain beauty and sparkle.

# Jade

| Unique Hazards | Torch Retipping | Torch Sizing | Pickling & Plating | Files & Abrasives | Polishing | Steamer | Ultrasonic |
|---|---|---|---|---|---|---|---|
| None | ✗ | ✓ | ✗ | ✓ | ✓ | ✓ | ✓ |

The term "jade" actually refers to two different stones: jadeite and nephrite. The more familiar of the two, jadeite is a mythical stone that often fetches huge prices at auction. Nephrite, on the other hand, is much less valuable than jadeite when comparing stones of similar size and workmanship.

Jadeite jade is an aggregate gem: It comprises tiny, closely packed, interlocking crystals. Traditionally, jadeite is associated with Eastern cultures, where it has been used in carvings and jewelry for the past few centuries. Like any popular gemstone, jadeite is often imitated by less valuable materials and enhanced through various methods to improve its appeal.

With a fibrous chemical structure, nephrite is the lesser-known and less-expensive form of jade. Nephrite is the type of jade that scholars refer to when they speak of China's "Jade Age," when tools and other day-to-day items were made of nephrite.

Green is the color most commonly associated with jadeite (Figure 1, top). However, it also comes in lavender, reddish orange, white, gray, and yellow. These colors can often combine to form patches within the same piece of jadeite. Such combinations have specific names, such as "Moss in Snow," which refers to green patches on a white background.

Nephrite is commonly found in a spinach-green color (Figure 1, bottom). It also comes in black, yellow, white, brown, and various shades of green. While it can be mottled like jadeite, nephrite is not known for having an uneven color.

Myanmar (formerly Burma) is considered the primary source for fine quality jadeite, especially the highly saturated, transparent green material that resembles emerald (and which has the greatest value). Nephrite jade can be found in Canada, New Zealand, China, and the United States.

## Enhancements

Jade is routinely coated with wax after polishing; this fills in any tiny gaps between the stone's individual crystals. An ultrasonic or a steam cleaner can occasionally remove or damage this wax and slightly dull what appeared to be a lustrous stone.

# Quick Tips

### Rock Solid Facts
- Mohs Hardness: 6 to 7
- Cleavage/Fracture: Granular

### Tools That Rule
- A laser welder for retipping with the stone in place.
- A safety-edge file to avoid scratching the stone.
- A lid for the pickle pot to avoid accidentally pickling the stone.
- A water bath or heat shield to protect the stone from a jeweler's torch during sizing.

### Bench Check
- Are the seats in a jade-set piece cut to fit the profile of the stone?
- Have you avoided pickle and acid-based plating solutions, which can etch the surface of jade?

### Features and Benefits
- Jade is extremely durable and can be worn for many years without special handling.
- Jade has a long history and appeals to our need for mysticism in our jewelry.
- Jade is available in many colors that appeal to various tastes.
- Jade exhibits many price points and can work in any budget.

# Picture This

> Replacing this relatively inexpensive jadeite would be difficult due to its unique shape.

< The left half of this dyed jadeite cabochon was heated briefly with a jeweler's torch.

> Jade is a very tough stone, but only moderately hard: The surface of this nephrite was still scratched by a jeweler's tool.

< This white jadeite cabochon was cut in half. The left side was soaked in warm, purple fabric dye and has changed color, illustrating how easily jadeite can be convincingly dyed.

Dyes are also common. A large portion of the jadeite found in nature is very light in color or white to gray, and these stones must be dyed to achieve bright green colors and lavender shades. Most of these dyes are fairly stable, but they can fade with age.

In addition, jadeite can be bleached and impregnated with polymers. This is known as "B" jade. Detection of this treatment is difficult and usually requires advanced laboratory testing. "B" jade looks like very high quality material, but is worth only a fraction of the value of untreated jade.

With the exception of wax coating, nephrite is not routinely treated, as the stone's low value does not warrant the cost of treatment.

## Clean It

Steam and ultrasonic cleaning are considered relatively safe for jade, but they can damage the wax coatings, especially when very strong detergents or very hot cleaning solutions are used. If you are dealing with extremely high quality jadeite or antique pieces, clean with lukewarm water, since a change in the condition of the wax may be noticeable and not restorable.

## At the Bench

Jade is relatively easy to handle at the jeweler's bench, although precautions do need to be taken against scratching the material with files and sanding tools. Use a safety-edge file when finishing prongs.

Jade will not tolerate heat from a jeweler's torch, and retipping cannot be done with the stone in place (unless a laser welder is used). However, sizings can be done with jade in place if a heat shield is used, or if the stone is submerged in a water bath.

After completing torch work, do not pickle an item set with jade. The pickle can etch the surface slightly, and it will definitely damage any type of wax coating. Pickle may also dull "B" jade (jadeite).

Setting jade in jewelry does not require specialized techniques. However, since most jade is in cabochon or carved form, you must cut seats in prongs or bezels that match the profile of the stone as closely as possible. This prevents the loosening of the jade over time. Don't use glue to prevent a jade from rattling in its setting: The glue is often visible and degrades over time.

## Care for Wear

Jade is a very durable stone and is less likely to chip or break than diamond. (Hardness, a resistance to scratching, is often confused with toughness, a resistance to breaking. Jade is tougher than diamond, not harder.) However, the owner should be advised to avoid exposing jade-set jewelry to harsh chemicals, such as strong household cleaners, as they can damage the wax coating and cause dulling to occur.

Jade pieces often can be worn for decades without issue. After years of heavy wear, customers should have their stones re-polished in order to restore their luster.

# Lapis Lazuli

| Unique Hazards | Torch Retipping | Torch Sizing | Pickling & Plating | Files & Abrasives | Polishing | Steamer | Ultrasonic |
|---|---|---|---|---|---|---|---|
| None | 💥 | ⊘ | 💥 | ⊘ | ⊘ | ⊘ | 💥 |

A fabled opaque blue gemstone, lapis lazuli comprises the minerals calcite, lazurite, and pyrite. Lazurite gives lapis its blue color, calcite is often seen as white patches in the stone, and pyrite imparts the gold flecks that shimmer in high quality lapis.

High quality lapis shows an even, bright blue color with very little or no white calcite patches. The pyrite flecks in the best qualities should be evenly distributed throughout the stone. Less valuable qualities have eye-visible patches of white calcite, clumps of pyrite, or very little pyrite. In the past several years, light blue material known as "denim lapis" has been marketed. Reminiscent of denim blue jeans, the stone's light blue color results from the high calcite content.

The finest quality lapis is traditionally from Afghanistan. Other sources include Pakistan, Chile, and the former Soviet states.

## Enhancements and Imitations

Lapis lazuli is often dyed to improve color. Dyeing consists of coloring the calcite patches blue to disguise their presence. This results in a stone that appears to be very high quality. To determine if a stone has been dyed, swab a discreet area of the stone (around a drill hole on a bead for instance) with acetone on a cotton swab (Figure 1). If certain types of dye are present, they will bleed onto the acetone-soaked swab. Because this swab test could noticeably damage the stone, we recommend using specialty swabs with hard, pointed ends; they are available through cosmetic stores as makeup applicators. These odd-looking cotton swabs allow much greater control of the placement of the acetone on the stone and reduce the risk of visible damage.

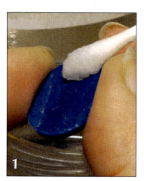

Acetone doesn't affect all dyes. In such cases, you must rely on observing the pattern of the dye within the natural calcite veins in the lapis. Dyed calcite will appear as dark bluish-violet veins traveling through the stone.

Lapis is routinely coated with wax after polishing; this fills in any surface pits and gives the stone a higher luster.

## Quick Tips

### Rock Solid Facts
- Mohs Hardness: 5 to 6
- Fracture: Granular (has a texture similar to the surface of a sugar cube)

### Tools That Rule
- A safety-edge file to avoid scratching or abrading the stone when finishing prongs.
- A water bath or heat shield to protect the stone during torch work.
- A lid for the pickle pot to avoid accidentally pickling the stone.

### Bench Check
- Do the seats fit the profile of the stone as closely as possible?
- Is as much metal as possible polished prior to setting the stone?

### Design Check
- Is a piece designed in a way where the stone is protected?
- Does the design allow for gentle cleaning techniques?

### Features and Benefits
- Lapis has a vivid blue color that is less expensive than comparable colors in other blue gems.
- Lapis is known as a masculine stone that is appropriate for wear in men's jewelry.

## Picture This

> This lapis cabochon, likely of Chilean material, has large patches of white calcite that could be dyed to give the stone an even blue color.

< This particular tablet of lapis has the typical pyrite inclusions. The unique shape of the stone and pattern of pyrite would make it difficult to replace if damaged.

> The abrasion on the corner of this lapis tablet occurred during the finishing process when a snap-on sanding wheel touched the stone. It has a granular texture that can be seen by the naked eye.

Due to its popularity, lapis has many imitators on the market. Chalcedony (particularly jasper) is sometimes dyed blue to imitate lapis. Sodalite is a blue stone usually found in Canada and often misrepresented as "Canadian lapis." Purpler in color than lapis, sodalite has white veins running through it that can cause many to confuse it with lapis. Both sodalite and dyed jasper chalcedony tend to have a higher polish than lapis, and both lack the pyrite inclusions.

Imitation lapis is manufactured in a laboratory setting and cannot be called synthetic because it is not chemically the same as natural lapis. This material is quite convincing: It has the even blue color of lapis with the expected pyrite flecks. However, it registers only about a 3 in Mohs hardness and can be scratched easily. To determine if a lapis is an imitation, rub the stone rapidly on paper. Imitation lapis will have a shiny area where it was rubbed. Do not rub a visible portion of the stone; do this only on an area hidden from view.

## Clean It

Since lapis comprises different minerals clustered together, the stone can easily crack or break. The mineral-based composition also makes lapis porous, so it absorbs liquids and oils. Therefore, avoid steam and ultrasonic cleaners,  especially since dyes may not be stable in either of these cleaning environments. In addition, harsh cleaning can easily remove a stone's wax coating and cause it to appear noticeably dull. Use warm water, very mild detergent, and a soft brush or cloth to clean lapis (Figure 2). After cleaning, dry it thoroughly to prevent the stone from absorbing the cleaning liquids.

## At the Bench

Lapis cannot tolerate heat. Direct torch contact will discolor the stone, making it turn gray, and induce thermal shock that will likely cause the stone to crack. If you cannot remove the stone, use a heat-shielding product or water bath to protect lapis during torch work.

Do not pickle lapis-set pieces, as discoloration and dulling may result. Plating solutions should also be avoided for this reason.

Files, burs, and sanding tools can easily leave noticeable scratches and chips on lapis. While safety-edge files can be used, caution must still be taken in the tool placement and pressure to avoid damaging the stone. Therefore, finish as much of the metal as possible prior to setting lapis to decrease contact between the stone and the tools.

Lapis is often fashioned in free-form cabochons or tablets, as well as custom carved shapes. And while lapis is not overly expensive when compared to other gems, it is difficult to replace uniquely shaped items when they are damaged. (Color matching can also pose a problem.) Therefore, make sure that seats cut into bezels and prongs fit the profile of the stone as closely as possible. This decreases the likelihood of breaking the stone while applying pressure during setting.

## Care for Wear

Lapis is fairly easy to wear. However, the owner should be advised to avoid exposing lapis-set jewelry to harsh chemicals, such as strong household cleaners, as they can cause discoloration and dulling to occur.

Stones worn daily in rings or bracelets can tend to dull over time. The stones can be easily re-polished to restore the original luster. Although quite rare, dyed items can occasionally "bleed" onto the wearer's clothes.

# Morganite

| Unique Hazards | Torch Retipping | Torch Sizing | Pickling & Plating | Files & Abrasives | Polishing | Steamer | Ultrasonic |
|---|---|---|---|---|---|---|---|
| None | 💥 | ⚠️ | ⚠️ | ⚠️ | ⚠️ | 💥 | ⚠️ |

While aquamarine and emerald are the most prominent members of the beryl family, jewelers will periodically encounter lesser-known varieties. They include morganite (pink), heliodor (golden or yellow), and goshenite (colorless). There's even a green beryl that doesn't quite qualify as emerald: Either it doesn't have the saturation needed, or it's more yellowish than the bluish green typically associated with that stone. (The two most delicate members of the beryl family, red beryl [bixbite] and maxixe [pronounced ma-she-she], are rare and seldom seen in jewelry.)

Of these lesser-known beryls, morganite is the stone we most frequently encounter in jewelry. However, yellow, green, and colorless beryls can be handled in the same manner at the bench.

Often overlooked as a moderately priced pink gem, morganite owes its name to J.P. Morgan, who was an avid gem collector. Morganite's color ranges from very pale to moderately saturated pink. Orangey pink or peach colors can fade with prolonged exposure to direct sunlight or some other constant heat source.

Most morganite is mined in South America, particularly Brazil. Other sources include Madagascar, Southern California, and Afghanistan.

## Enhancements

Morganite comes out of the ground with an orangey pink or peach color. It is often heat treated to remove any yellowish component, resulting in a pure pink or more purplish pink. (The same thing is done to aquamarine to remove the yellowish component that naturally occurs in its color.) This treatment is considered stable. It is not detectable.

## Clean It

Like aquamarine and emerald, morganite commonly has liquid-filled inclusions. If heated, these inclusions could expand faster than the surrounding gemstone, causing a fracture. Consequently, neither ultrasonic nor steam cleaning is recommended for morganite. If you do use an ultrasonic, the cleaning fluid should be just hot enough that you can put your fingers into it comfortably. If you steam clean morganite, you may very well shatter the stone.

The safest way to clean morganite is with a brush and warm, soapy water. You can also dip the brush in the ultrasonic cleaning solution and use it to clean the gem.

## Quick Tips

### Rock Solid Facts
- Mohs Hardness: 7.5 to 8
- Cleavage/Fracture: Conchoidal

### Tools That Rule
- A safety-edge file to avoid scratching or abrading the stone during prong finishing.
- A water bath or heat shield to protect the stone from a jeweler's torch during sizing.
- Room-temperature pickle to prevent thermal shock to the stone.

### Bench Check
- Have you verified the identity of the stone?
- Are seats cut properly to avoid stone breakage?
- Is as much metal as possible polished prior to setting the stone?

### Design Check
- Is your piece designed in a way that will allow easy access to clean a morganite without use of ultrasonic or steam cleaners?

### Features and Benefits
- When pink is in fashion, morganite offers a way to carry it over to jewelry at a moderate price.
- Morganite is often cut into unique shapes that appeal to many tastes.

## Picture This

> Too much pressure was applied to this morganite during prong setting, resulting in a chip.

< A photo of the same stone without magnification. This is not a result that is easily explained to customers.

## At the Bench

Before performing any bench work, verify that a gemstone is actually morganite. This is important since the stone is often mistaken for another pink gem, kunzite (Figure 1, left). Kunzite will fade with exposure to light and heat, and it has two cleavage directions—a nightmare for many stone setters. Morganite can also be mistaken for pink sapphires and pink spinels, as well as their synthetic counterparts. However, these stones require minimal special handling in comparison to kunzite or morganite. Once you identify the gemstone, you can take the appropriate precautions.

Since morganite is often cut into custom or unique shapes, it can be difficult to replace—even if the problem is aggravated by the subtle differences in the intensity and exact hue of the pink color among morganite stones. Care should be taken—even with very light and inexpensive stones—to avoid breakage and the whole time-consuming issue of replacement.

When performing repairs with morganite-set jewelry, remember that none of the beryls can tolerate heat, let alone heat from a jeweler's torch. Therefore, morganite must be removed from settings for retipping and other torch work that must be done close to the stone. Sizings can usually be accomplished by placing the morganite in a water bath or using a heat-shielding product. Avoid quenching a morganite piece in very hot pickle, as the sudden temperature change can cause liquid inclusions to expand and crack the stone. Pickle in room-temperature solution to avoid this potential problem.

Though morganite is relatively hard, you must still be careful when using files and abrasives for prong finishing. A safety-edge file is highly recommended for prong shaping done with the stone in place. It is also advisable to finish as much polishing as possible before setting the stone. Since diamond- and corundum-based abrasives will scratch the surface of morganite, avoid them when performing work with the stone in place.

When stone setting, make sure that the seats are cut properly and match the outline of the stone. This is especially important with unique shapes and custom cuts, as any rough or raised areas in the seat can cause a pressure point that results in stone breakage.

## Care for Wear

Morganite requires minimal special care from the wearer, but they should be made aware that morganite worn daily in a ring will probably require re-polishing in a few years. Customers should also be aware that morganite's peach color might fade over time with exposure to heat and light. As with most light-colored gems, the accumulation of soap scum and lotion on the underside of the stone greatly decreases its beauty; therefore, regularly scheduled professional cleaning is recommended.

# Opal

| Unique Hazards | Torch Retipping | Torch Sizing | Pickling & Plating | Files & Abrasives | Polishing | Steamer | Ultrasonic |
|---|---|---|---|---|---|---|---|
| Porous. Absorbs oils and chemicals | 💥 | ❌ | ❌ | ❌ | ❌ | 💥 | 💥 |

With its fiery display of colors, opal is unique among gemstones. Contrary to popular belief, opal's ever-changing color results not from water trapped in the stone, but rather from light diffraction. Opals consist of arrangements of submicroscopic silica spheres, and the size and arrangement of these spheres cause light to diffract at differing focal depths—producing the flashes of color that fascinate so many. (While this structure gives opals their often-incredible displays, it can also result in porousness.)

Known for being fragile stones, opals can be easily chipped, cracked, and broken. To complicate matters, opals are not always what they seem; they may be completely solid, or they may be assembled. For instance, "boulder" opals—thin seams of opal still attached to the ironstone on which the opal formed—are often mistaken for two types of assembled opals: "doublets" (a thin layer of opal glued to a backing) and "triplets" (a thin layer of opal sandwiched between a backing and a clear top). The reverse also holds true—and since doublets and triplets are much more fragile, the mistake could have disastrous consequences. If you are not sure if the opal you are dealing with is a doublet/triplet, assume that it is assembled and treat it as such.

Most opal is mined in Australia. Other sources include Nevada and Mexico.

## Enhancements

Opals can be enhanced in a few different ways. One method of treatment is to subject the opal to smoke. Due to opal's porous nature, the carbon in the smoke penetrates the opal's surface, and causes a light opal to appear dark. If a smoked opal is chipped, the thin layer of dark color can easily be seen.

A similar effect can be obtained through sugar treatment. In this treatment, an opal is placed in a sugary liquid (such as fruit juice) so that the sugar can soak into the surface of the stone. The opal is then carbonized with acid to impart a thin, dark layer of color. This treatment is considered permanent. However, if a treated opal is chipped, the underlying color can be visible.

## Clean It

Since opals are sensitive to changes in temperature, cleaning them in hot ultrasonic or steam cleaners poses great risks: It could cause cracking or worsen existing cracks. The vibration of ultrasonic cleaners can also cause problems: If an opal is already loose in the setting, an ultrasonic may rattle the stone enough to cause damage. In addition, the chemicals used in ultrasonics can attack the glue that holds an opal doublet or triplet together. (The same is true of heat from a steam cleaner.) Therefore, the safest method for cleaning an opal, assembled or not, is with a soft to medium brush and warm, soapy water. After cleaning, dry the stone thoroughly to prevent it from absorbing the cleaning fluids. To prevent damage, always inspect the opal under magnification for existing cracks or glue before undertaking any type of cleaning.

# Quick Tips

### Rock Solid Facts
- Mohs Hardness: 5 to 6.5
- Cleavage/Fracture: No cleavage

### Tools That Rule
- A laser welder for repairs with the stone in place.
- A water bath or heat shield to protect the stone during torch work.
- A hydro-torch has a concentrated flame that can be directed to very specific areas, minimizing the chance of overheating the stone.
- A lid for the pickle pot to prevent accidentally pickling the stone.

### Bench Check
- Have you finished as many parts as possible previous to setting the stone?
- If retipping, have you removed the stone?

### Design Check
- Can the design be changed to make the setting less stressful?
- Can multiple prongs be used instead of a few heavy prongs?
- Is the stone protected by the mounting from most sharp blows?
- Can a softer alloy be used without compromising the design?
- Can the opal in your design be easily removed if a repair is necessary in the future?

### Features and Benefits
- Opal's moving patches of color and ever-changing appearance make it unique among gemstones.
- Knowing a one-of-a-kind opal formed in Australia can add to the stone's appeal.
- Rings show opal's colors to their best advantage with every movement of the hands.
- If heavy wear is avoided, an opal can be enjoyed for a lifetime.
- Opal is recognized as one of the October birthstones.

## At the Bench

With their extreme fragility and porousness, it may seem that opals are a jeweler's worst nightmare. However, implementing simple precautions and adopting specialized techniques can avert the majority of problems.

Heat presents one of the greatest challenges: the bench jeweler working on an opal. The stone simply cannot tolerate the heat from a torch or the rapid temperature changes caused by heating and subsequent cooling. Even heat from the friction of polishing can sometimes damage an opal.

Heat generally becomes an issue in repair work as opposed to manufacturing operations (where the opal can be set after all torch work is done). When possible, remove the opal from the setting before beginning any repair (Figure 1). If removal is not feasible, immerse the opal in water or use a heat-shielding product before heating the metal. Keep in mind that some metals conduct heat more readily than others and can complicate heat shielding. For example, sterling silver conducts heat very effectively and can make shielding an opal and achieving a solid solder joint difficult. Platinum, however, is not nearly as effective a conductor of heat, even though it requires higher temperatures.

Avoid using a file or bur next to an opal by doing as much of the sanding and polishing work as possible before setting the opal.

When setting an opal (Figure 2), do not use glue to secure the stone unless you're doing inlay work. Using glue makes removal of the opal for a future sizing or repair very difficult, if not impossible.

## Picture This

> This opal assemblage consists of natural and synthetic opal pieces glued together and backed in black stone. The close-up on the right clearly shows the bubbles created by the glue used to hold the piece together. Placing a stone like this in any kind of solvent or heat will cause it to fall apart.

< Some opals tend to craze or crack without any outside influence. Often, crazing becomes much more noticeable when a stone is removed from a closed-back mounting. Crazed opals are highly prone to breakage, so it is important to carefully check for crazing before removing a client's stone from its mounting.

> These photos show a black opal doublet (note the backing on the bottom) with its crazed top, and a crazed common white opal.

< This is a profile of an opal triplet. The clear top cap is visible.

> This type of setting is a good technical solution to setting an opal. By scalloping the bezel, less pressure is needed to push the bezel around the stone snuggly, reducing the chance of breakage. This particular opal is smoke treated.

< This sugar-treated opal has been chipped. It is easy to see the very thin layer of dark color on the surface of the stone, which contrasts strongly with the actual white body color.

Solvents only aggravate the problem, since immersing an expensive opal in solvent can worsen existing cracks. We have seen situations where the setting had to be literally peeled away, piece by piece, from the stone. The result: We had to build the whole piece over.

Last but not least, don't put an opal in pickle. Pickle is usually hot and could cause thermal shock, cracking the stone. The acid of the pickle can also accelerate any cracking or crazing that is already present.

## Design It

When making a custom piece of opal jewelry, design it in a way that protects the opal. For example, a freeform design may have raised areas of metal around the opal that would block most blows. These raised areas are not necessarily the actual bezel or prongs, but buffers protecting the opal (Figure 3). This concept is especially recommended with rings. Of course, some designs (or customers) do not allow for this added safety measure, but it is an idea to consider whenever possible.

3

Choose setting styles that not only minimize the pressure applied to the stone, but also reduce the stone's exposure to files and hammering during the setting process. Also, select soft metals that can be easily bent over the stone. For example, a thin bezel of 18k yellow gold requires less pressure to push over the stone than a thicker bezel of 14k yellow. To further reduce setting pressure, use a series of small prongs with thin profiles as opposed to four heavy prongs. (If thick prongs must be used, be sure the jeweler anneals them to soften the metal and then pre-bends the prongs to reduce the amount of leverage needed to bring them down on the opal.)

## Care for Wear

One of the great myths about opals is that they should be oiled to retain their shine. The problem here is that opals are porous, and many oils oxidize over time. Very often a well-meaning opal owner puts oil or even a cosmetic moisturizer on her opal. The opal absorbs minute amounts of the substance. The absorbed substance oxidizes or discolors over time, leaving the opal an unattractive dingy yellow.

If the customer insists on some type of oil treatment, tell her that keeping an opal in water is fine but not necessary. Mineral oil is probably the least harmful oil to put on the stone, but again it is not necessary.

Opals are soft, so everyday wear will abrade the surface and cause dullness. To help an opal retain its shine, recommend that clients wear opals only for special occasions. A client who insists on wearing an opal daily should know that the opal will require re-polishing in the future.

## EXTRA FACETS
# Metal Interactions With Stones

Although this is a book devoted to handling gemstones at the bench, we felt a few pointers about the working properties of common metal alloys would be helpful in avoiding stone damage. However, always contact your metal supplier and confirm the characteristics of the alloys that you use.

**14k yellow gold** serves as the alloy to which the working properties of other alloys are usually compared.
- Moderate resistance to scratching and wear.
- Good malleability; moderately easy bending (important for prongs and bezels).
- Easy to polish.
- Overall, moderately desirable for stone setting.

**14k nickel white gold** is a common white gold alloy in the United States, but is meeting some resistance due to nickel allergies and difficulties presented by its brittleness.
- Good resistance to scratching and wear; prongs last longer than 14k yellow gold.
- Hard; springy during bending.
- Brittle and prone to breaking and cracking.

**14k palladium white gold** is gaining in popularity but is slightly higher in cost than 14k nickel white gold.
- Less memory than nickel white gold; prongs stay where they are placed.
- More malleable than nickel white gold; easier to bend over stones.
- More difficult to cast successfully than other 14k alloys.

**18k yellow gold** is the high-end standard for yellow gold in the United States.
- High malleability; easy to bend over stones; less pressure needed to bend.
- Loses its polish more quickly than 14k yellow gold.
- Prongs lift more easily than 14k yellow gold; may present a stone security issue for the abusive jewelry wearer.

**18k nickel white gold** is the high-end white gold standard in the United States.
- Brittle and prone to cracking or breaking.
- Very hard; bead setting takes physical strength and patience.
- Difficult as a stone-setting metal.

**Platinum 950/Cobalt** is used primarily as a casting alloy.
- Brittle in comparison with other platinum alloys; may crack when bending.
- Not overly desirable for stone settings due to brittleness.
- Welding very difficult, if not impossible.

**Platinum 900/Iridium** is the standard platinum alloy used in the United States.
- Considered excellent for stone setting.
- High malleability makes bending metal over prongs easy.
- High resistance to wear.
- Work hardening prongs increases wear resistance.

**Platinum 950/Iridium** has been gaining popularity in recent years.
- Very high malleability allows for easy stone setting.
- Scratches easily.
- Issues of stone security may arise if settings are not properly work hardened.
- Deformation of jewelry items due to low hardness; channel setting may not maintain stone security.

**Platinum 950/Ruthenium** is preferred for machined and die-struck products such as wedding bands.
- Rigid and difficult to bend over stones during setting.

**Heat-treatable gold and platinum alloys** have the benefit of added hardness after treatment. However, use caution when heat treating these alloys with stones in place. Check with the supplier for instructions for heat treating and do not heat treat if the setting contains stones that will not tolerate the process.

# Pearl

| Unique Hazards | Torch Retipping | Torch Sizing | Pickling & Plating | Files & Abrasives | Polishing | Steamer | Ultrasonic |
|---|---|---|---|---|---|---|---|
| Porous, absorbs oils and chemicals; etched by acid (pickle) | ✗ | ✗ | ✗ | ✗ | ✓ | ✓ | ✗ |

Both natural and cultured pearls form when an irritant gets lodged inside a mollusk. The mollusk then deposits layers of nacre (very fine crystals of calcium and aragonite) over the irritant and produces a pearl. In a natural pearl, the irritant may be any organic or inorganic matter. In cultured pearls, the irritant is a mother-of-pearl bead and/or a piece of mollusk mantle tissue placed in the mollusk by a technician. The mollusk covers the nucleus with alternating layers of conchiolin (a protein-like substance similar to human nails) and nacre. Since it is very soft, nacre can be scratched or chipped easily.

Both cultured and natural pearls include freshwater and saltwater varieties. These names simply mean that the pearl formed in either a freshwater or a saltwater mollusk. The information outlined in this chapter pertains to working with all pearls.

## Treatments

Many pearls of light body color have been bleached to improve color matching. Pearls can be dyed to almost any color; bright pinks, purples, greens, yellows, and blues are common. Exotic colors, such as bronze or black, can be achieved through irradiation.

Dyes tend to concentrate around drill holes (Figure 1) or blemishes, while irradiation often turns the conchiolin layer of cultured pearls dark. To help identify either of these treatments, look down drill holes under magnification.

In the case of very high-end pearls, coatings have been an issue. These coatings—used to improve the luster of high-end pearls—are difficult to detect because they are not visible to the naked eye. Since microscopic examination is also not always accurate, use a qualified laboratory if you suspect a pearl has been coated.

## Clean It

Don't clean pearls in an ultrasonic: The vibrations of the machine can harm the nacre, especially around drill holes that have chipped nacre rims. Also, the chemicals used in the ultrasonic can attack the conchiolin layer, which can cause cracking over time. Steam cleaning is likewise not recommended: The temperature can damage the organic proteins in the pearls.

The best way to clean pearls is in clear water with a soft brush (Figure 2) and a mild detergent, followed by a thorough rinse. If the pearls are strung at the time of cleaning, lay them flat to dry; hanging them will cause the silk cord to stretch, leaving gaps between each pearl.

## Quick Tips

### Rock Solid Facts
- Mohs Hardness: 2.5 to 4
- Cleavage/Fracture: None

### Tools That Rule
- Crystal cement or clear nail polish for stringing.
- Silk and French wire for stringing.
- Solvent-based epoxy to secure the pearl. (Water-based epoxy doesn't hold as well.)
- Methylene chloride solvent for removing pearls.
- A pearl drill or pearl jig for accurate drilling.
- A water bath or heat shield to protect the pearl during torch work.
- A lid for the pickle pot to prevent accidentally pickling the pearl.

### Bench Check
- Is as much metal as possible polished prior to setting the pearl?
- Is the end of the pearl strand finished with French wire or double wrapped?
- Is epoxy being used for easier removal in the future?
- If retipping, have you removed the pearl?
- If restringing, have you washed your hands?

### Design Check
- Can the pearl in your design be easily removed if a repair is necessary in the future?
- Is the pearl protected by the mounting from most sharp blows?

### Features and Benefits
- Pearls are infinitely versatile and go with any outfit.
- Pearls are classic and always in style.
- Pearls are available in many price ranges that fit most budgets.
- Pearls come in a wide range of colors that appeal to nearly any taste.
- Pearl is recognized as one of the June birthstones.

## At the Bench

Pearls cannot tolerate heat or chemicals. In any repair situation requiring heat close to the stone, remove the pearl. If the pearl cannot be removed, use a heat-shielding product or immerse it in water before doing any torch work. Also, do not quench in pickle solution, which will etch the pearl's surface. Instead, allow the pearl to air-cool.

Most pearls set in jewelry have been drilled and glued onto a post with epoxy. Soaking the piece in methylene chloride solvent will usually loosen the pearl for removal. If methylene chloride solvent does not work, acetone can be used as a last resort. However, acetone may dull the surface of the pearl slightly, especially if the pearl soaks in it for several hours.

An alternate method for removing a pearl is to place the piece in a small pan of water, then heat the water. When the water is warm, try to pull the pearl from the post. Repeat this every minute until the water is too hot to touch. If epoxy was used to secure the pearl, this method of removal usually works. But if a glue containing cyanoacrylate, such as Superglue, has been used, acetone often is required. This presents a very nasty situation in the case of an expensive pearl: Cyanoacrylate products can stain the conchiolin and cause noticeable damage to the pearl. The possible risks of acetone removal should be discussed with the customer prior to any repair that requires it.

Setting a pearl in a piece of jewelry may require drilling or half drilling the pearl. A pearl jig is useful for this procedure. It keeps the drill bit perpendicular to the surface of the pearl while holding both the drill and the pearl steady. Another option is a pearl drill, which reduces the chipping that can occur with a chattering drill bit or a moving pearl. After the pearl is drilled, use epoxy to attach it to the post. Epoxy allows the pearl to be removed without the use of harsh solvents if a repair is necessary.

Since pearls are very soft, buffing compounds used for metal

## Picture This

> No damage is evident on this freshwater pearl (left). However, after being soaked in pickle, this same pearl appears chalky and has lost its luster (right).

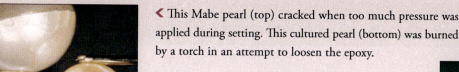

< The drill hole on this cultured pearl is chipped. This shows a lack of care in drilling the pearl.

> The nacre of this pearl was damaged by over-aggressive drilling.

< This Mabe pearl (top) cracked when too much pressure was applied during setting. This cultured pearl (bottom) was burned by a torch in an attempt to loosen the epoxy.

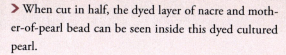

> When cut in half, the dyed layer of nacre and mother-of-pearl bead can be seen inside this dyed cultured pearl.

< The areas of different luster, which appear as discolorations, are the result of buffing this black cultured pearl with rouge. This is not something that can be easily explained to a customer.

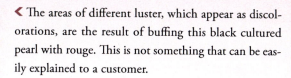

> This cultured pearl features a cup hook to which a clasp will be attached. This is not an appropriate method for applying a clasp to fine pearls.

polishing can often leave nasty surface marks. Therefore, polish any piece prior to setting a pearl.

## Design It

Take a pearl's delicacy into account when designing a piece of jewelry. Pearls set in earrings or necklaces do not experience a great deal of stress. Pearls set in rings, however, are subject to abrasions in daily wear, as well as soaps and lotions that can cause discoloration. Therefore, design a ring so that the metal rises above the pearl and blocks some of the potential impacts.

## Stringing

Not every jeweler wants to string pearls. However, given the large number of pearl strands available for sale, not to mention those already in customers' hands, knowing how to string is almost a necessity.

In stringing, a few rules must be followed. First, saltwater pearls and large freshwater pearls should be strung on silk, with knots in between each pearl (Figure 3). The knots keep the pearls from rubbing against each other and prevent loss of the whole strand if the cord breaks. In the case of very small pearls, where knots in between each pearl may look unsightly and bulky, you can tie a knot every 5 to 10 pearls.

Second, the ends of the strands should be finished with French wire or a double wrap of the silk cord (Figure 4, top). When double wrapping, secure the cord by coating the wrap with crystal cement or clear nail polish.

Pearls should be restrung when the knots between them are no longer white, which can be every two years if the pearls are worn daily. When restringing pearls, count the pearls in the customer's presence and inform her that the pearl strand will be slightly shorter after restringing. (This is usually because silk stretches out from wear.)

Finally, it is critical that the stringer's hands be clean, since an unwashed hand can turn the string gray or black (Figure 4, bottom).

## Care for Wear

As one of our fathers, a second-generation jeweler, says, "Pearls are like a mink coat. They are the last thing you put on before going out and the first thing you take off when you get home." This is a very wise statement. Advise your customers to put their pearls on last, after the perfume, soap, lotion, hair spray, and makeup have been applied. These cosmetics can attack the porous surface of the pearl over time, leaving the pearls dull and lifeless. No amount of cleaning can bring back the original luster that cosmetics etch away from a pearl's surface. After wearing their pearls, owners should wipe the body oils off the pearls with a soft cloth to keep them from absorbing the oils and eventually dulling.

# EXTRA FACETS
# Organic Gems

| Unique Hazards | Torch Retipping | Torch Sizing | Pickling & Plating | Files & Abrasives | Polishing | Steamer | Ultrasonic |
|---|---|---|---|---|---|---|---|
| Very soft; can dissolve in acids | 💥 | 💥 | 💥 | ✓ | ✓ | 💥 | 💥 |

Organic gems owe their existence to living organisms: Shell is the outer casing of mollusks, coral is a marine structure formed from the secretions of tiny polyp-like organisms, and amber is the fossilized sap of ancient trees. Jewelers create cameos, carvings, beads, and cabochons from coral and shell, and usually form amber into beads and cabochons.

All organic gems are extremely fragile, and bench jewelers should treat them with the utmost caution. This is especially true if they are set in antique jewelry, as is often the case with shell cameos and coral. (Jewelers should always approach antiques with extreme caution, since removing metal patinas or adding components can greatly decrease a piece's value.) Organics are extremely heat sensitive, and even indirect heat from the torch can cause damage. Water baths and heat-shielding products can be used, but they only partially offset the risk of damage. Organics are also very soft and can be easily scratched, so be sure to complete any filing, finishing, or polishing before the stone is set. In addition, do not place the stones in pickle or acid-based plating solutions, which can quickly destroy organics.

Due to their fragile and porous nature, coral and shell should be cleaned with distilled water and a soft brush. With antique cameos or elaborate coral carvings, any type of detergent residue could cause discoloration or a change in surface texture. Less porous than other organics, amber can be cleaned with lukewarm, soapy water. However, ultrasonic and steam cleaners should be avoided: Organics are not bonded together as tightly as crystal materials and cannot tolerate the heat and vibration of cleaners.

Organics are too fragile to stand up to day-to-day wear. Advise customers to avoid wearing organic-set jewelry when washing hands, as soap can damage them. As with pearls, direct your customers to put their organic gems on last, after the perfume, lotion, hair spray, and makeup have been applied, since these substances can cause harm. In addition, owners should wipe the body oils off the stones, as oils and perspiration can damage organics over time. To help protect their stones, recommend that customers wear their organics for special occasions only.

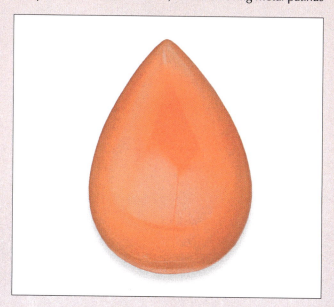

# Peridot

| Unique Hazards | Torch Retipping | Torch Sizing | Pickling & Plating | Files & Abrasives | Polishing | Steamer | Ultrasonic |
|---|---|---|---|---|---|---|---|
| Etched by acid (pickle) | 💥 | ⬭ | 💥 | ⬭ | ⬭ | ⬭ | ⬭ |

Peridot is the best-known yellow-green gemstone and the August birthstone. An affordable gem, it has not been mired in controversy over treatments, and its history is free of negative connotations like those surrounding conflict diamonds.

The primary source of peridot is the San Carlos Indian Reservation in Arizona, where it provides a source of income to the tribe. This unique source can be a strong selling point for the gem, especially for clients who wish to buy American products. Other sources include Myanmar (formerly Burma) and Pakistan, both of which produce some of the richest hues of peridot.

## Enhancements

Peridot is not routinely treated to improve its appearance. It is this lack of known treatment that makes peridot a good choice for customers concerned about owning enhanced gemstones.

## Clean It

Although peridot is relatively durable, ultrasonic and steam cleaners should be used with caution. Before cleaning, examine the stone under magnification, as peridots can have liquid inclusions that could be damaged by heat or vibration. If you see inclusions, revert to cleaning with a soft brush and warm, soapy water. If you opt for an ultrasonic cleaner (perhaps because a piece has accent diamonds that are not easily cleaned using less risky means), do not leave the peridot in the cleaner for more than 5 to 10 minutes.

We generally do not recommend steam cleaning peridot. If you wish to steam clean, don't hold the stone directly in the most concentrated part of the steam jet. As a gauge, hold the jewelry between your fingers: If the metal is too hot to hold, then the jewelry is too close to the concentrated portion of the steam jet.

## At the Bench

While peridots are one of the less delicate colored stones to work with at the bench, they are extremely sensitive to acids. Do not pickle a peridot, as the acid pickle solution will etch the surface of the stone. Also, keep

## Quick Tips

### Rock Solid Facts
- Mohs Hardness: 6.5 to 7
- Cleavage/Fracture: Conchoidal

### Tools That Rule
- A safety-edge file to avoid scratching or abrading the stone during prong finishing.
- A laser welder for repairs with the stone in place.
- A water bath or heat shield to protect the stone during torch work conducted away from the stone.
- A lid for the pickle pot to avoid accidentally pickling the stone.

### Bench Check
- Have you avoided pickle and acid-based plating solutions, which can etch the surface of a peridot?
- If retipping, have you removed the stone?

### Design Check
- Can the peridot be removed if a repair is necessary?
- Is a piece designed in a way where the stone is protected?

### Features and Benefits
- Affordable prices make peridot a good alternative to other, more expensive green gems.
- Peridot is not known to be routinely treated.
- Peridot is recognized as the August birthstone.

## Picture This

› This is the same peridot before (top) and after (bottom) being subjected to strong pickle. In the top image, the stone's surface has a bright luster. In the bottom image, the stone has a hazy appearance, and polish lines and scratches are much more visible.

‹ This photo shows a magnified view of the culet of a peridot viewed through the table of the stone. Abrasions of the facet junctions can be easily seen. Also, note the doubling of the images of the abrasions. This is a characteristic of peridot.

in mind that some plating solutions are acid based and can harm a peridot as much as an acid pickle. Avoid plating with the stone in place (Figure 1) or make certain that your plating solution is safe for peridot. If in doubt about a solution, contact the manufacturer.

Peridots are heat sensitive, so avoid directly heating it with a jeweler's torch. Retipping with the stone in place is not possible unless using a laser welder. However, sizings and other repairs that are not performed close to the peridot can be done if the stone is protected with a water bath or heat-retardant product.

Prongs can be finished with a safety-edge file. Nonetheless, you should do as much finishing and shaping as possible prior to setting the stone. Peridots do chip and abrade much more easily than sapphires or rubies, and can be damaged by harsh polishing compounds applied liberally or with too much pressure.

## Design It

Since peridots do abrade with regular daily wear, you must design custom peridot jewelry pieces in a way that protects the stones from sharp blows. While necklaces, pins, and earrings are usually not plagued with issues of abrasion, rings and bracelets can be subject to severe wear. However, if a stone can be easily replaced after several years of wear, it may not be necessary to overcompensate with the design to avoid abrasion. If the peridot has a very unique cut or a high-end color, then precautions are more advisable. For example, set a unique peridot in a piece with raised metal that will absorb most impacts in daily wear.

## Care for Wear

Customers need to understand that peridots can abrade over time with heavy wear, and that peridots and chemicals do not mix well. Advise clients to take peridot jewelry off before using chemical products.

# Quartz

| Unique Hazards | Torch Retipping | Torch Sizing | Pickling & Plating | Files & Abrasives | Polishing | Steamer | Ultrasonic |
|---|---|---|---|---|---|---|---|
| None | 💥 | 🚫 | 🚫 | 🚫 | 🚫 | 🚫 | 🚫 |

When most people envision quartz, they think of a clear crystal. However, the quartz family actually comprises stones of various colors, particularly three popular and versatile gems.

**Amethyst** is the purple variety of quartz. Its color results from iron impurities in the crystal. In general, the darker and more saturated the color, the more valuable the stone. However, stones that are so dark as to appear black are of lesser value. Quality amethyst is relatively free of inclusions.

Much of the world's supply of amethyst is mined in South

America (particularly Brazil) and Africa. Generally, there is a plentiful supply of various qualities and sizes of amethyst on the market. The abundant supply contributes to affordable prices and makes amethyst a favorite among customers and custom gem cutters.

Also colored by iron, **citrine** is the yellow variety of quartz (Figure 1). Like amethyst, it is plentiful on the market in many sizes and qualities, including high quality material that is free of inclusions and has a saturated color. The yellow of citrine can vary from a very light lemony color to a rich orangey yellow. Trade names like Madeira are often used to describe different subtleties of color.

A third popular variety of quartz is **ametrine** (Figure 2), a combination of amethyst and citrine in the same crystal. As with its single-colored quartz cousins, ametrine is found in large sizes that are relatively inclusion-free. The two colors present in a single crystal make ametrine popular among custom gem cutters.

## Enhancements

While quartz is not routinely treated, the iron atoms in citrine and those in amethyst can be altered by heat and irradiation. Thus, heating an amethyst causes it to turn yellow (or into a citrine) and irradiating a citrine turns it purple (or into an amethyst). In fact, much of the citrine on the market today started out as amethyst and was heat-treated. Neither treatment is detectable.

## Quick Tips

### Rock Solid Facts
- Mohs Hardness: 7
- Cleavage/Fracture: Conchoidal, splintery or uneven

### Tools That Rule
- A safety-edge file to prevent chips and abrasions when finishing prongs.
- A laser welder for repairs with the stone in place.
- A water bath or heat shield to protect the stone during torch work.
- Room-temperature pickle to avoid thermal shock.

### Bench Check
- Have you checked the stone for bulging pavilions or thick girdles before setting, and cut the seats appropriately?
- If retipping, have you removed the stone?
- Do you have a plan to avoid stone breakage during setting?

### Design Check
- Can the quartz in your design be removed easily if a repair is necessary?
- Does the mounting protect a custom-cut stone from sharp blows?

### Features and Benefits
- Large sizes available for dramatic designs.
- Affordable prices for every budget.
- Wide range of colors for many tastes.
- Amethyst is recognized as the February birthstone.
- Citrine is recognized as one of the November birthstones.

## Clean It

Ultrasonic and steam are generally considered safe methods of cleaning quartz. However, you should avoid sudden changes in temperature. Don't use an ultrasonic cleaner if it is too hot to comfortably put your fingers in it. (*Note:* Do **not** put your fingers in a vibrating ultrasonic, as it can damage tendons.)

Also, when steam cleaning, do not put the stone in the direct path of the most concentrated area of the steam jet. As with peridot, we find that holding the jewelry between our fingers while steam cleaning keeps us from putting it into this danger zone (Figure 3). When dealing with a custom-cut stone that can be difficult to replace, play it safe and clean quartz jewelry with a soft brush and warm, soapy water.

## At the Bench

Amethyst, citrine, and ametrine are relatively easy to work with at the bench. The most common problems faced by jewelers result from cut quartz shapes. Standard cuts often have bulged pavilions and thick girdles, and custom cuts vary widely, all of which can make setting a challenge. Therefore, when setting quartz, carefully observe the particular variations of the cut. Prongs and stone seats must be carefully shaped to accommodate thick girdles or other variations. Lack of attention to these details can contribute to stones breaking during the setting process.

Perform retipping on quartz jewelry with the stone removed, as quartz will not tolerate heat from a torch—it will simply shatter. Using a laser welder for retipping is a wonderful option if access to a laser exists. (Make sure the beam doesn't hit the stone, or damage could occur.) Sizing and similar repairs can be done with the stone in place if a water bath or heat shield protects the stone. However, heat amethyst jewelry gradually to avoid a color change.

Most quartz can withstand pickle solution. However, since a sudden temperature change can cause thermal shock, you must allow a quartz-set item to air-cool before placing it in room-temperature pickle.

Although quartz is fairly hard, steel files and diamond- and corundum-based abrasives can damage it. Finish prongs with a safety-edge file to avoid chips and abrasions. Also take precautions to avoid contacting the stone with abrasive wheels or papers that can dull the surface.

## Design It

Although replacing a standard cut of amethyst, citrine, or ametrine may not present financial hardship, replacing a custom cut can be difficult. If you are designing a piece around a unique cut, engineer the piece in a way that protects the stone from wear. For example, a uniquely cut stone may have a pointed top. Therefore, you would want to design the piece so that the pointed top will not be subjected to sharp blows during daily wear.

## Care for Wear

In the case of amethyst, exposure to continuous heat, like that of the sun through a window, can cause its purple color to fade over time. Make sure that customers are aware of this. You may also want to keep this in mind when planning your store displays: Keep amethyst away from very hot lights.

## Picture This

> These two citrines are typical of the odd designs often cut from quartz. Take special care during setting to avoid breaking the corners of such stones.

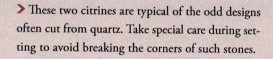

< This unfortunate amethyst was the victim of excessive pressure and an uneven seat during setting. Also note its bulged pavilion; this further necessitates cutting a proper seat to accommodate its proportions.

> The uneven bulged pavilion on this citrine (top) makes cutting a seat slightly more time consuming, since the seat must be matched with the stone's uneven outline (bottom) and bulge to prevent the stone from breaking.

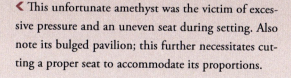

< This amethyst has a very thick girdle and a vertical fracture that could be problematic if too much pressure is applied during the setting process.

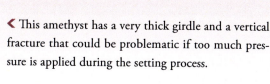

# Ruby

| Unique Hazards | Torch Retipping | Torch Sizing | Pickling & Plating | Files & Abrasives | Polishing | Steamer | Ultrasonic |
|---|---|---|---|---|---|---|---|
| Overheating firecoat etches the surface | | | | | | | |

The pre-eminent red stone in most people's minds, ruby is the red variety of the mineral corundum. A versatile stone due to its beauty and durability, it is one of the few gemstones that can withstand heat from a jeweler's torch.

A ruby's country of origin can have an effect on its market value. However, establishing country of origin is not always possible, and some noted gemological laboratories will not attempt to identify sources. Historically, Burmese rubies have been considered the finest, and stones that can be definitively identified as coming from Myanmar (formerly Burma) can command a premium on the market. However, just because a ruby is from Myanmar does not mean it is automatically attractive. Very nice rubies can also be found in Thailand, Vietnam, and Africa. Qualities of ruby do vary at each source.

## Enhancements

Heat treatment is the most prevalent and stable enhancement used on rubies. In traditional heat treatment, the stones are packed in flux or borox and subjected to varying temperatures in controlled heating atmospheres to improve their color and clarity. Specific types of heat treatment can produce stars in certain rubies that would otherwise not be attractive in their untreated state.

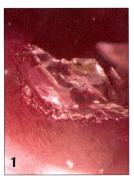
1

A less common form of color improvement is diffusion treatment, in which color-causing chemicals are melted onto the surface of the ruby. Although this treatment is fairly durable, any chipping or deep abrasions can remove the color layer and result in highly visible damage. A gemologist can provide invaluable help in detecting this enhancement.

Another treatment involves filling cavities in rubies with a glass-like substance (Figure 1, shown under magnification). A jeweler must be especially alert to this enhancement, as the filler material can melt with exposure to a torch. Cavity filling can also be considered a bit deceptive: Rubies are sold by weight, and

# Quick Tips

## Rock Solid Facts
- Mohs Hardness: 9
- Cleavage/Fracture: Conchoidal (parting in star stones)

## Tools That Rule
- A safety-edge file to avoid abrasions during prong finishing.

## Bench Check
- Have you avoided overheating the stone and burning firecoat onto its surface?
- Are your seats cut in a way that accommodate bulged pavilions?
- Have you checked to see if the ruby is untreated?

## Features and Benefits
- Ruby is the classic red stone, which makes it a popular choice.
- Ruby is durable and can be worn on a regular basis in a variety of jewelry, including rings.
- Ruby is recognized as the July birthstone.

# Picture This

> This ruby is the victim of too much heat from the jeweler's torch. The result is the dull, ugly patches that firecoat has burned onto the surface.

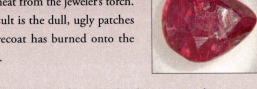

< This ruby shows abrasions that have occurred at facet junctions. This type of damage can happen as a result of daily wear or the sloppy use of tools, such as files, during setting.

> The huge fracture in this ruby was caused by overheating with a torch. A crystal in the stone expanded and fractured the surrounding ruby.

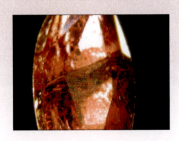

some of the filled cavities can be quite large and represent a significant percentage of that weight. However, cavity filling can be a byproduct of the heat treatment process and not necessarily an intentional attempt at subterfuge. Filled cavities can be detected by looking for a luster difference on the surface of the stone. If you are unable to discern whether a ruby has been filled or not, consult a gemologist.

## Clean It

Most rubies can be safely cleaned in an ultrasonic or steam cleaner, which will not affect heat and diffusion treatments. However, neither of these cleaning procedures should be used on glass-filled rubies, as the fillings can vary and are not always stable when exposed to sudden changes in temperature or vibrations. Instead, use a brush and warm, soapy water.

## At the Bench

Compared with other gemstones, ruby is quite easy to deal with at the jeweler's bench. Although some reference books do not recommend heating a ruby directly with a jeweler's torch, we feel that most rubies, with the exception of glass-filled stones, can withstand such heat. Retipping can be done with the stones in place if you use common sense and caution. One of the few potential problems is overheating the stone, which can cause the firecoat to etch the surface. Good torch technique, in which the flame is not overly concentrated on the stone, can help you avoid overheating and prevent this ugly problem (Figure 2).

Also, be on the lookout for untreated fine quality ruby. It brings a premium on the market, since it has not been subjected to any type of high heat treatment. That also means it requires special care at the bench, as the heat from a torch can actually change the stone's characteristics and, in effect, heat treat the ruby. If you are dealing with a very high-end stone, make sure you do not heat it with a torch unless you are absolutely certain that heat treatment has occurred. Instead, remove it from the setting for retipping or use a laser welder if possible. During sizings and other torch work performed near the stone, use a heat shield to protect an untreated ruby.

Most rubies can withstand pickle solution. However, you must allow a ruby-set item to air-cool before placing it in the pickle, as the sudden temperature change can cause thermal shock or spontaneous cracking. Glass-filled rubies should never be pickled, since damage can occur to the filling.

As with any colored stone, you should use a safety-edge file to finish prongs. Although ruby is very hard and quite tough, abrasions can still happen if care is not taken during finishing. Most polishing compounds are safe to use on ruby-set pieces. However, aluminum oxide–based compounds have a hardness very similar to that of ruby, and the possibility of damage to a stone is not worth the risk of their use. Read polishing compound labels carefully to avoid any issues.

## Design It

Rubies often have bulging pavilions that can make cutting seats more challenging for the bench jeweler. Thicker mountings often need to be used; they give the jeweler more metal to modify to accommodate the bulge (Figure 3).

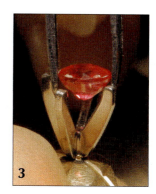

## Care for Wear

Rubies require very little special care: Quite hard and tough, they are suitable for daily wear. As with any stone, though, they will appear dull when dirty. Therefore, recommend regular professional cleanings to your customers.

# Sapphire

| Unique Hazards | Torch Retipping | Torch Sizing | Pickling & Plating | Files & Abrasives | Polishing | Steamer | Ultrasonic |
|---|---|---|---|---|---|---|---|
| Overheating firecoat etches the surface | | | | | | | |

When most people think of sapphire, the color blue comes to mind. Sapphires, however, encompass all of the different color variations of the mineral corundum, with the exception of red. (If corundum is red, it is called ruby.) Sapphires in colors other than blue are generally referred to as fancy sapphires. Among the most popular fancy colors are pink and yellow. The fabled and elusive Padaparascha is a pink-orange color named for the lotus flower.

Sapphires are found in many areas around the world, predominantly Southeast Asia, Australia, Africa, and the Indian subcontinent. Historically, the finest blue sapphires have come from the Kashmir region between India and Pakistan. Sri Lanka (Ceylon) is known for producing light blue stones with high saturation. Thailand is said to have darker blue colors, and Myanmar is known for highly saturated darker blues. Fancy colors come from most of the known sources.

## Enhancements

Sapphires, particularly blue stones, are routinely heat treated to improve either color or clarity; this treatment is stable and requires no special handling. It is sometimes done in conjunction with the glass filling of cavities. We see glass filling most commonly in pink and purple sapphires. Glass-filled cavities are problematic when exposed to the jeweler's torch, as the filling can melt or change color and texture. Therefore, you must learn how to recognize a glass-filled stone. (Glass-filled stones can be identified with a microscope, and some can be identified with a loupe. Filled cavities can be detected by looking for a luster difference on the surface of the stone. The filling can also contain gas bubbles. If in doubt, contact a gemologist for an accurate identification.) If you suspect a sapphire has been filled, remove the stone prior to any torch work.

Blue sapphires are commonly subjected to diffusion treatment. In traditional diffusion treatment, titanium and iron are placed on the surface of the stones, which are then heated. These color-causing chemicals diffuse into the sapphire's surface, resulting in a thin layer of rich blue color. While this treatment is stable when exposed to a jeweler's torch, if a treated stone is chipped, abraded, or seriously scratched, the color layer can be removed, leaving a visible colorless area. To detect the treatment, view stones in diffused white light or while they are covered in water, wintergreen oil, or methylene iodide. The most obvious sign of treatment is concentrations of color along the facet junctions (Figure 1).

Similar to the traditional method described above, another form of diffusion treatment uses beryllium instead of titanium and iron. Also known as bulk or lattice diffusion, it is used to produce the famed pink-orange Padaparascha color from pink sapphire. Nearly any other color of sapphire can also be improved

# Quick Tips

### Rock Solid Facts
- Mohs Hardness: 9
- Cleavage/Fracture: Conchoidal (parting in star stones)

### Tools That Rule
- A safety-edge file to avoid abrading facet junctions.

### Bench Check
- Have you checked for glass-filled cavities?
- Have you avoided overheating the stone and burning firecoat onto its surface?
- If retipping, have you removed untreated stones?
- Are your seats cut in a way that accommodates bulged pavilions?

### Design Check
- Does your design feature a thicker mounting to accommodate a bulged pavilion?

### Features and Benefits
- Sapphires are available in nearly every color to suit any taste.
- Sapphires are durable and can be worn regularly.
- Sapphires have a wide variety of price points that can accommodate any budget.
- Sapphire is recognized as the September birthstone.

or changed using this treatment. This form of diffusion appears to be stable when exposed to a jeweler's torch. It is also not seriously affected by chips and abrasions because it extends farther under the surface than traditional diffusion treatment. Because research into this new form of treatment is ongoing, we recommend keeping up with trade magazines to stay current on the research.

## Clean It

Sapphires can be safely cleaned by steam and ultrasonic. Heat and diffusion treatments (both traditional and bulk) are not harmed by either of these cleaning methods. The main precaution with cleaning is in regard to glass fillings, since the filling material can vary and is not always stable to sudden changes in temperature or vibrations. The safest way to clean glass-filled stones is with a soft brush and soapy water.

## At the Bench

A durable stone, sapphire is relatively easy to deal with at the jeweler's bench when compared with other stones that are very soft or heat sensitive. Although many references recommend avoiding torch work with sapphires altogether, we feel that settings can be safely retipped with the stone in place—if common sense is used. It is important to use good torch techniques to avoid overheating the stone, which can cause pitting and firecoat etching. Some bench jewelers avoid getting firecoat on the stones themselves and paint it only on the metal. Experiment with a few inexpensive sapphires of your own to help determine if firecoat causes a problem for you.

Sapphires with glass fillings should not be heated directly with a torch, as the filling may melt. If a stone is glass-filled, use a water bath or heat shield to protect it while doing torch work that is not close to the stone. If protecting the stone is not possible, remove it before doing any work.

Untreated sapphires can be inadvertently heat treated by a jeweler's torch. If you are dealing with a stone that has not been treated, such as the Kashmir sapphires in antique pieces, do not heat the stone directly with a torch: Doing so may take away the characteristics that give the stone added value. Remove any such stone from the mounting before retipping. In situations where removing the stone is not feasible, we recommend using a laser welder.

While sapphires can withstand pickle solution, let a sapphire-set item air-cool before placing it in the pickle, since the sudden temperature change can cause thermal shock or spontaneous cracking. However, glass-filled sapphires should never be placed in pickle, as etching of the filler can occur.

Although sapphire is very hard, abrasions of facet junctions can occur when you're finishing prongs, so use a safety-edge file. Traditional diffusion-treated sapphires are particularly ugly when damaged by a file or cup bur; the color layer can be removed by the abrasive nature of the tool.

Aluminum oxide–based polishing compounds have a hardness similar to that of sapphire, so it's slightly possible they could damage a sapphire-set piece. To avoid any problems, read polishing compound labels carefully.

The colors of most sapphires are stable, with the exception of some yellows that can fade with exposure to light and heat. When dealing with a yellow sapphire, place the stone in direct sunlight for a few days to make sure that no fading occurs. Be sure that the yellow sapphires you "test" in this manner are your own stones. Altering the appearance of a customer's stone in this manner is not going to help build your reputation as a professional.

## Picture This

> This sapphire has been overheated while firecoat was on its surface. The resulting dull circles on the table can be removed only through repolishing.

< The sapphire on the left shows no evidence of traditional diffusion treatment. The stone on the right has color concentrations on facet junctions that prove traditional diffusion treatment. The diffusion-treated stone must be handled with extreme care to avoid surface abrasions or chips, which will be very visible due to the light inner color of the stone becoming visible.

> The sapphire on the left shows an extreme example of a bulged, deep, and unsymmetrical pavilion, and will prove more difficult to set than the stone on the right.

## Design It

Sapphires are often cut with very bulged pavilions that make cutting seats quite challenging. Using a thicker mounting (Figure 2) will give the jeweler more metal to modify to accommodate the bulge of the stone.

## Care for Wear

Hard and tough, sapphires can be worn on a regular basis, and do not require special precautions. However, advise your customers that traditional diffusion-treated stones should be worn with the utmost care, as chipping, scratching, and abrading can remove the color layer and result in ugly damage. Re-cutting a damaged stone that has undergone traditional diffusion treatment is not an option, since even more of the color layer will be removed.

## EXTRA FACETS
# Iolite

| Unique Hazards | Torch Retipping | Torch Sizing | Pickling & Plating | Files & Abrasives | Polishing | Steamer | Ultrasonic |
|---|---|---|---|---|---|---|---|
| None | ☠ | ⚠ | ⚠ | ⚠ | ⚠ | ⚠ | ⚠ |

Found in India, the violet-blue gem iolite is often confused with the more expensive tanzanite and, to a lesser degree, blue sapphire. Like tanzanite, iolite is highly pleochroic. However, while tanzanite's colors range from blue to violet, iolite has a blue to nearly colorless pleochroism. However, unlike tanzanite, there is no significant difference in value between lighter- and darker-colored stones.

Although iolite is relatively inexpensive, care should still be taken at the bench since it is somewhat delicate. (Iolite measures 7 to 7.5 on the Mohs hardness scale.) Because this gem does not tolerate heat from a jeweler's torch, use a water bath or heat-shielding product if the stone cannot be removed from the setting prior to sizing or similar repair. The fact that iolite is often set in sterling silver exacerbates this danger, since silver is very conductive and transfers heat rapidly. Iolite also has a single perfect cleavage direction that makes chipping the stone highly probable if too much pressure is applied during the setting process. Acids can damage iolite, so avoid pickle and acid-based plating solutions.

Cleaning iolite is best done safely with warm, soapy water and a medium to soft brush. However, if you choose to live dangerously and clean an iolite-set piece in an ultrasonic, be certain that you are willing and able to replace the stone if damage occurs. The same situation is true of steam cleaning iolite. Although using the ultrasonic or steam cleaner usually will not cause damage to the stone, fractures due to thermal shock can occur from time to time.

Iolite requires minimal special care from the wearer. However, stones can be scratched with heavy wear. Make sure the client understands that iolite is not an appropriate stone for the gym or the garden. With light-colored stones, the accumulation of soap scum and lotion on the underside of the stone can greatly decrease its beauty. Therefore, you should recommend that the owner schedule regular cleanings.

# Spinel

| Unique Hazards | Torch Retipping | Torch Sizing | Pickling & Plating | Files & Abrasives | Polishing | Steamer | Ultrasonic |
|---|---|---|---|---|---|---|---|
| Synthetic spinel triplets cannot tolerate heat and acid-based solutions | ⊘ | ✓ | ✓ | ⊘ | ✓ | ✓ | ✓ |

Although spinel and ruby are often found together in the same mines (mostly in Southeast Asia), spinel usually takes a backseat to the revered corundum. However, because both gemstones have similar colors and properties, they were often considered the same material before the technology for gem identification was developed.

Quite brilliant when cut, spinels come in many colors. Reds, pinks, purples, and orangey reds are the most common hues. Blues are also available, but they tend to have a strong grayish component to their color, as do most other colors of spinel.

## Enhancements

Spinel is unique in that there are no known treatments performed on it to enhance color or clarity. This can be a very good selling point for customers who have aversions to treated gemstones.

Synthetic spinel is available and is often used to simulate amethyst, peridot, and emerald. To simulate the birthstones, two colorless pieces of synthetic spinel are glued together using a colored glue. To detect these assembled triplets, look for the separation of the two pieces of synthetic spinel that form the top and bottom of the gem. This separation is visible with magnification.

## Clean It

Spinel is one of the most durable colored gemstones. It can routinely undergo steam and ultrasonic cleaning without ill effects.

Although spinel is durable, approach cleaning synthetic spinel triplets with caution. Steam and ultrasonic cleaners can destroy the glue layer. The safest method of cleaning is to use a soft to medium brush with warm, soapy water.

## At The Bench

Spinel is relatively easy to work with at the jeweler's bench. Torch work can be done in close proximity to the stone, but care must be taken to keep the stone itself cool. However, some jewelers report that natural, lighter-color spinels fade when exposed to torch heat. Thus, sizings and similar procedures are probably safe with a natural spinel in place (Figure 1), but you should remove the stone before retipping.

> ## Quick Tips
>
> ### Rock Solid Facts
> - Mohs Hardness: 8
> - Cleavage/Fracture: Conchoidal
>
> ### Tools That Rule
> - A safety-edge file to avoid abrasions during prong finishing.
>
> ### Bench Check
> - Have you identified a synthetic spinel triplet before beginning any work?
> - Have you removed natural spinels from their settings before retipping?
> - Have you allowed a spinel-set piece to air cool before placing it in pickle?
>
> ### Features and Benefits
> - Spinel's durability makes it a good choice for everyday wear.
> - Spinel is a wonderful purchase for the gem enthusiast who already has the basic, more recognized colored stones.
> - Spinel is not treated and appeals to clients who do not want to purchase enhanced gemstones.

However, synthetic spinel triplets, which are often used in class rings and mothers' rings, cannot tolerate the heat from a torch. If subjected to heat, the glue holding the triplet together can melt, causing the top and bottom stones to slide apart.

Spinel-set jewelry can be pickled. However, you should pickle

## Picture This

> These four spinels show a range of color. Three have the typical grayed-out spinel color, but the stones are lively nonetheless.

< Though quite hard, spinel can abrade, as this rather extreme example shows. This particular stone was worn daily in a ring for several decades.

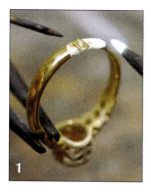

the piece after it has air-cooled to avoid the remote possibility of thermal shock and the shattering of the stone. Synthetic spinel triplets cannot tolerate pickle or other acid-based solutions, since the acid could attack the glue and cause the stones to separate. Acids can also change the color of the glue.

Although spinel is very hard in comparison to most other gemstones, precautions should be taken to avoid abrading the stone with finishing tools. To prevent damaging facet junctions, use a safety-edge file to finish prongs. Also, be especially careful with diamond- and corundum-based abrasives, as they will damage the surface of a spinel.

## Care for Wear

Spinels are quite good for daily wear; no special precautions must be taken. Regular professional cleanings help spinel maintain its sparkle. Although spinel is very durable, owners of large, high-quality natural spinel need to be made aware that replacing the stone exactly may prove difficult if it is damaged; this is due to spinel's lack of popularity in the market, which means there are fewer examples of high-end stones. The positive side is that the owner of a high-end spinel can be assured of the gemstone's uniqueness.

Although quite durable, synthetic spinel triplets can be damaged. Over time, the chemicals in soaps, lotions, and shampoos can degrade the layer of glue in a triplet. It would be wise to inform your customers that showering with their jewelry on should not be considered a form of jewelry cleaning.

# Tanzanite

| Unique Hazards | Torch Retipping | Torch Sizing | Pickling & Plating | Files & Abrasives | Polishing | Steamer | Ultrasonic |
|---|---|---|---|---|---|---|---|
| Very easily scratched | ✗ | ✗ | ✗ | ✗ | ✗ | ✗ | ✗ |

Tanzanite is named after Tanzania, the country in which the stone was discovered in the 1960s. The stone's unique combination of blue and purple results from pleochroism, a property of some gemstones in which different colors are visible in different crystal directions. If the stone is cut skillfully, all of the colors can be seen. A stonecutter may also choose to orient the cutting of a tanzanite so that it appears more blue or more purple.

Tanzanite has a wide range of qualities and appearances. Stones are expected to be eye clean and are usually clean under microscopic examination. Color is the deciding factor in determining the value. In general, the more blue the stone, the higher its value. High quality stones have a deeply saturated color with a velvety richness. Lightly colored stones are less valued. When buying loose tanzanite, be careful of stones that are cut very deep or have excessive pavilion bulge or depth; extra depth is a way to increase the stone's color saturation, but it can also make setting difficult. However, we advise against having a very deep tanzanite re-cut for easier setting, since the color could change and reduce the stone's value.

Tanzanite's short history on the market has been volatile. There have been peaks of very high prices due to increased demand as well as tragic mine accidents that have interrupted production. These peaks have been offset by periods of very low pricing due to overproduction and false media accusations of links with terrorist organizations.

## Enhancements

The vast majority of tanzanite comes out of the ground a yellow-brown color with slight hints of violet. The stones are then heat treated to create the rich blues and purples that have made tanzanite one of the most popular gems on the market today. This treatment is considered permanent and stable.

## Clean It

A delicate stone, tanzanite is easily chipped or scratched. Many tanzanites also contain liquid-filled inclusions. These two factors mean that the stone requires special handling during cleaning. Ultrasonic cleaners are not recommended, as the heat can cause thermal shock and the ultrasonic vibrations can fracture the stone. Although damage due to ultrasonic cleaning is rare, and many jewelers routinely clean tanzanites in this way, you should avoid risking a very expensive or uniquely cut stone that would be difficult to replace.

Steam cleaners and tanzanite are also not the best of combinations, since tanzanite can suffer from thermal shock and fracture. As with ultrasonic cleaning, problems with steam cleaning are rare but not unheard of, but the potential problems are not worth the risk.

So how *can* you clean a tanzanite? We prefer to use a soft brush and warm water. You can also dip a tanzanite-set piece in the ultrasonic when the machine is off and the solution is not so hot that you can't put your fingers into it comfortably. If the solution is too hot for your fingers, the change from ambient temperature may be enough to cause thermal shock to the stone.

## Quick Tips

### Rock Solid Facts
- Mohs Hardness: 6 to 7
- Cleavage/Fracture: One direction of perfect cleavage

### Tools That Rule
- A safety-edge file to avoid abrasions during prong finishing.
- A laser welder for repairs with the stone in place.
- A water bath or heat shield to protect the stone from torch heat during sizing.
- A flex-shaft equipped with small polishing buffs and disks for a last-minute polish that won't damage the stone.

### Bench Check
- Are all the prongs shaped prior to setting the stone?
- Are the seats in your tanzanite piece cut properly to avoid stone breakage?
- Is as much of the metal as possible polished prior to setting the stone?

### Design Check
- Can the tanzanite in your design be removed if a repair is necessary in the future?
- Does the mounting protect the tanzanite from most sharp blows?

### Features and Benefits
- Tanzanite's unique blue-violet color appeals to many customers.
- Tanzanite's exotic country of origin adds mystique.
- Tanzanite is recognized as one of the December birthstones.

## At the Bench

Due to tanzanite's fragile nature, the stone is very easy to abrade, scratch, or chip during the setting process. When hammering or tightening a tanzanite (Figure 1), use great care and develop a habit of regularly checking for proper

fit and metal contact with the stone as you go. If a setting features thick, hard prongs, take care to cut the seats correctly so as not to create pressure points (Figure 2).

Abrasions and scratches often occur during the final prong shaping. Therefore, shape the prongs as much as possible before setting the stone. Once the stone is set, finish any shaping with a safety-edge file.

Tanzanite's softness also makes it vulnerable to polishing compounds. Pre-polish as much of the mounting as possible before setting the stone. For the final polish, use a flex-shaft with small polishing tools, as they offer greater control and decrease the possibility of hitting the stone (Figure 3).

Like most gems, tanzanite cannot tolerate heat from a jeweler's torch. Retipping with the stone in place is not possible unless using a laser welder. Removing the stone is the safest course of action for sizing and other torch repairs. If removal is not possible,

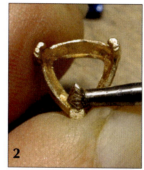

place the stone in water or cover it with a heat retardant before attempting any torch work.

## Design It

When designing tanzanite jewelry, choose metal alloys that are more malleable, such as platinum or 18k yellow gold, because they require less pressure to bend over the tanzanite, thus reducing the chance of damage. Also, use multiple small prongs instead of a few heavy prongs to lessen the pressure needed to bend the prongs over the stone.

Make sure your design protects the stones from sharp blows or abrasions caused by wear. Rings, in particular, subject stones to stress, so creating a design that has the metal raised above the stone to bear the brunt of the abuse can prolong the life and beauty of the tanzanite.

## Care for Wear

A tanzanite ring worn regularly will abrade over time. Therefore, the safest course of action is to reserve tanzanite rings for special occasions. If the wearer does not want to limit wear, the stone can be re-polished after a few years to restore its sparkle. When wearing tanzanite jewelry, your customers should avoid lotions and soap, which can be difficult to remove without using a steam or ultrasonic cleaner.

Pendants, earrings, and pins are generally subjected to less stress than rings. However, these pieces should be removed during showering or hair washing to prevent shampoos, conditioners, and soaps from sticking to the stones.

## Picture This

> This tanzanite was chipped in an attempt to push a heavy prong over the stone. This is not a chip that can be covered by a prong, and re-cutting the stone will result in a noticeable loss of size. The pavilion view shows the extent of the chip.

< The abrasions on the facet junctions of this tanzanite are the result of daily wear in a ring. The scratches on the facets may be a result of sloppy finishing or of daily wear.

> The corner of this tanzanite was chipped during setting. In addition, a fracture resulted that runs diagonally through the stone. This stone is a total loss.

# Topaz

| Unique Hazards | Torch Retipping | Torch Sizing | Pickling & Plating | Files & Abrasives | Polishing | Steamer | Ultrasonic |
|---|---|---|---|---|---|---|---|
| Cleavage—avoid direct pressure | | | | | | | |

Commonly yellow, orange, or brown, natural topaz can also be found in a variety of other colors. Pink topaz is a lesser-known but appealing color of this well-known gemstone, and Imperial topaz has a pink-orange color that is reminiscent of zinfandel wine. However, due to the successful irradiation of colorless or unattractive light yellow topaz, many jewelers picture a greenish blue stone when they think of this gemstone.

Topaz is found in many areas around the world, with South America and Sri Lanka leading production.

## Enhancements

The most common treatment is the irradiation of colorless or very light yellow topaz to cause a blue color. This process is safe, as any residual radiation quickly dissipates. There is so much blue irradiated topaz available today that the different shades have trade names, such as Swiss blue or London blue, to denote slight variations in hue.

Recently, topaz that has been diffusion-treated or coated with thin film technology has found its way onto the market. These treatments can give an iridescent appearance to the stone or change the color altogether (Figure 1). Blue and green are currently the most common colors, but brown, red, and yellow are also possible. Bench jewelers must recognize these treatments, as the coatings can be damaged by steam and ultrasonic cleaners. To determine if a stone has been treated, use diffused back lighting to check for flaking of the coating. Some stones can also have what will appear to be a greasy surface. If you are in doubt about a stone, contact a gemologist.

## Clean It

Topaz is relatively durable, but it often has rather large liquid inclusions and one direction of perfect cleavage. Though many jewelers routinely clean topaz through ultrasonic and steam, doing so may damage stones with fractures or liquid inclusions. The steam cleaner is more likely to cause damage due to the possibility of thermal shock. However, an ultrasonic cleaner can also cause thermal shock if the cleaning fluid is very hot. In addition, the vibration of an ultrasonic can chip or crack the stone.

If you choose to live dangerously and steam clean topaz, do not put the stone in the direct path of the most concentrated area of the steam jet. We find that holding the jewelry between our fingers while steam cleaning keeps us from putting it into the hottest area; if the metal is too hot to hold, then the jewelry is too close to the concentrated portion of the steam jet.

If dealing with a rare pink or Imperial topaz, a custom-cut stone, or a diffusion-treated or coated stone, the safest course of action is to clean the jewelry with a soft brush and warm, soapy water.

## Quick Tips

### Rock Solid Facts
- Mohs Hardness: 8
- Cleavage/Fracture: One direction of perfect cleavage

### Tools That Rule
- A safety-edge file to avoid chipping or abrading the stone during prong finishing.
- A laser welder to allow stones to be left in place during repairs.
- A water bath or heat shield to protect the stone from torch heat during sizing.

### Bench Check
- Have you identified the stone as a topaz?
- Have you checked to see if the topaz is coated?
- If retipping, have you removed the stone?
- Do you have a plan to avoid stone breakage during setting?
- Is as much of the metal finished as possible prior to setting the stone?

### Design Check
- Can the topaz in your design be removed if a repair is necessary in the future?
- Is the piece designed in such a way that easily allows cleaning with a soft brush?
- Is a high end or custom-cut topaz in a ring protected by the mounting from most sharp blows?
- Have you used malleable metals and thin prongs in your design to reduce the pressure needed during stone setting?

### Features and Benefits
- Topaz provides a big look for any budget.
- Topaz is available in a wide range of colors that appeal to nearly any taste.
- Topaz is available in unique cuts and shapes for customers who want something "different."
- Topaz is recognized as one of the December birthstones.

## At the Bench

The primary issue with topaz that jewelers must remember is its one perfect cleavage direction. Hammering or putting pressure on a topaz runs the risk of cleaving the stone into pieces. This can result from even routine stone tightening on a prong-set topaz. To minimize this risk, cut stone seats with care and smooth away any burrs left by tools.

Although topaz is fairly hard, files and burs can scratch the stone. The most common tool damage on a topaz takes the form of small chips along facet junctions, again due to the cleavage. To avoid this, use files with safety edges and do as much sanding and filing as possible prior to stone setting.

Like most gems, topaz cannot tolerate heat from a jeweler's torch. Retipping with the stone in place is not possible unless using a laser welder. Sizings and other repairs can be done with the stone protected in a water bath or heat-shielding product. It is safest to remove the stone if possible.

Diffusion-treated or coated topaz must be handled with the utmost care, since the coatings can be worn off or otherwise affected by buffing compounds. Pre-polish as much of an item as possible prior to stone setting.

Smokey quartz can be mistakenly identified as topaz. Although there may not be a big difference in value between the stones, there are big differences in their physical properties.

## Design It

When designing a piece of topaz jewelry, be sure to take into account the stone's tendency to cleave. Use slightly thinner stone settings or more malleable alloys, and avoid overly thick prongs. Channel settings pose a special challenge, since pushing the girdle edge of the stone into the channel is a perfect opportunity to cleave the stone.

Setting designs should also be engineered in a way that protects the topaz from any sharp blows during normal wear. Whenever possible, design a piece so that the mounting takes the brunt of most wear-related blows.

## Care for Wear

Topaz is a relatively easy stone to wear, but customers should be made aware of the same issue as the bench jeweler: cleavage. Sharp blows, especially to rings and bracelets, often result in a broken topaz. Make sure the client understands that topaz is not an appropriate stone for the gym or the garden.

Otherwise, topaz will remain unfazed by the day-to-day use of detergents, cosmetics, and most household cleaning chemicals. The exception is diffusion-treated or coated topaz, which should be worn with the utmost care to avoid damage.

## Picture This

> This facet junction was abraded by a file during setting.

< This topaz was cleaved in half during a setting procedure gone bad. The break is smooth and flat, indicating that it is a result of the stone being hit in its cleavage direction.

> This coated topaz was polished with a buffing compound using the typical amount of pressure, for the typical amount of time. Notice how the coating has been polished away on the right side.

< The result after a moderate amount of pressure was applied to the small cleavage.

> This coated topaz shows a red color not typical of the stone. Its fuzzy appearance results from the coating being worn off.

# Tourmaline

| Unique Hazards | Torch Retipping | Torch Sizing | Pickling & Plating | Files & Abrasives | Polishing | Steamer | Ultrasonic |
|---|---|---|---|---|---|---|---|
| Watermelon and particolored stones cannot tolerate heat and pickle |  |  |  |  |  |  |  |

Commonly thought of as a green gem, tourmaline is actually available in nearly every imaginable color, although greens and pinks seem to dominate the market. The gemstone is found worldwide, with major sources in Brazil, Afghanistan, Africa, Sri Lanka, and the United States.

Types of tourmaline are usually denoted by their colors or by their places of origin. The following is a list of better-known tourmalines that are not named explicitly for their body color:

**Paraíba:** a neon blue to green type colored by copper and found in Paraíba, Brazil. (Although rare, some Paraíba are violet.)

**Rubellite:** a red tourmaline.
**Chrome:** a rich green tourmaline colored by chromium.
**Watermelon:** tourmaline crystal with a red core and green rim.
**Parti-colored:** tourmaline that shows two colors along the length of the same crystal.

## Enhancements

Tourmalines are sometimes treated with heat or irradiation to improve color. The treatment used depends on the color of the gem. Lightly colored stones are commonly irradiated to produce red (or rubellite), which tends to bring higher prices than many of the other colors. This treatment is not detectable, but it should be mentioned to clients as a high probability nonetheless.

Very dark stones may be lightened with heat treatment. As with irradiation, this treatment is undetectable but should be mentioned to customers as a possibility.

## Clean It

Tourmaline, especially rubellite and Paraíba, can have numerous liquid-filled inclusions. This can pose problems, as liquid inclusions expand more rapidly than the surrounding gemstone when heated. Thus steam cleaning becomes a very risky undertaking with tourmaline, and it should be avoided. Ultrasonic cleaning is also not advisable. Keep in mind that the more included a tourmaline is, the riskier cleaning becomes.

But many of us still want to live dangerously. If you can't resist the urge to use a cleaner, a cool ultrasonic is the safest. However, avoid cleaning highly included, watermelon, and parti-colored tourmalines in this way, since they may break at the boundaries between colors. As for the steamer, just say no.

## At the Bench

Despite the fact that tourmaline is fairly hard and tough, its liquid inclusions require special considerations. Because direct heat cannot be used on the stone, retipping with a tourmaline in place is not possible unless a laser welder is used. Heat shields and water baths can be used to cover the tourmaline during sizing. However, this must be done with the utmost caution, especially on highly included and parti-colored stones; even seemingly acceptable amounts of heat on these stones can cause fractures.

---

## Quick Tips

### Rock Solid Facts
- Mohs Hardness: 7 to 7.5
- Cleavage/Fracture: Conchoidal

### Tools That Rule
- A safety-edge file to avoid abrading the stone.
- A laser welder for repairs with the stone in place.
- A water bath or heat shield to protect the stone.
- Room-temperature pickle to avoid thermal shock.

### Bench Check
- Are the seats in your tourmaline piece cut properly to avoid stone breakage?
- Is as much of the metal polished as possible prior to setting the stone?
- If retipping, have you removed the stone?

### Design Check
- Is your custom design built in a way that allows easy cleaning of the tourmaline's pavilion without the use of an ultrasonic or steam cleaner?
- Have you chosen a malleable metal for setting that allows setting of long, narrow stones with the minimum of stress?

### Features and Benefits
- Tourmaline can be found in a color to suit any taste.
- Tourmaline can fit any budget.
- Tourmaline is recognized as one of the October birthstones.

---

As with other heat-sensitive stones, avoid placing tourmaline-set jewelry in hot pickle; use room-temperature pickle if necessary. However, you may want to avoid pickling watermelon and parti-colored tourmaline pieces entirely, as they tend to be very sensitive to any form of stress at the color boundaries. These particular stones are also hard to replace with exact duplicates, so every possible precaution should be taken.

Stone setting and prong finishing of tourmaline jewelry requires the usual precautions, with a few special considerations. Use a safety-edge file to avoid abrading and scratching the stone.

Also, finish as much of the mounting as possible prior to setting; this will help to eliminate possible stress on the stone. Again, be especially careful with parti-colored and watermelon tourmalines.

Tourmaline is often cut into long, rather narrow shapes with steep pavilion angles that can be prone to breakage when subjected to the pressure of stone setting. This "tourmaline cut" is common due to the elongated shape of the crystals and the gem cutter's attempt to compensate for strong and often dark pleochroic color in the crystal. To compensate for this, be sure that seats are cut properly; they should closely match the often steep pavilion angles of the stone to avoid pressure points that can cause breakage.

Treat Paraíba tourmalines with extreme caution at the bench. Although most colors and types of tourmaline are fairly moderate in price, Paraíba tourmaline can easily reach $10,000 per carat in the wholesale market. Replacing this stone is further complicated by a lack of supply and noticeable differences in color.

## Design It

When making a custom design using tourmaline, keep in mind that steam and ultrasonic cleaning are not acceptable. Design the piece in a way where most of the pavilion surface can be cleaned with a brush (Figure 1). Avoid close-backed designs to help with future cleaning issues. Also, using a malleable metal, such as platinum or 18k yellow gold, in prongs and bezels can help to lessen the pressure necessary to physically set the stone.

## Care for Wear

Most tourmalines require little in the way of special care for daily wear. Clients should understand that exposure to high heat is not recommended. If worn in a ring on a daily basis, stones will become abraded and lose their polish over the course of several years.

Watermelon and parti-colored tourmalines should especially be worn with caution. Avoiding impacts to the stone is critical, as these tourmalines often tend to break at the boundaries between colors. Customers need to be fully informed that such stones are not good for daily wear, especially daily wear in rings.

## Picture This

> This watermelon tourmaline shows the typical red core and green rim.

< This photo shows the tendency of watermelon and other parti-colored tourmalines to fracture on the color boundaries.

> The small chips around the perimeter of this green tourmaline resulted from careless wear. The large chip on the lower left is a result of a heavy-handed attempt to tighten the stone.

< This parti-colored tourmaline shows many reflective, jagged liquid inclusions that can cause tourmalines to fracture when the liquid expands with heat exposure.

> This profile view shows an extreme angle that is often encountered in the "tourmaline cut."

# Turquoise

| Unique Hazards | Torch Retipping | Torch Sizing | Pickling & Plating | Files & Abrasives | Polishing | Steamer | Ultrasonic |
|---|---|---|---|---|---|---|---|
| Very porous; Etched by acid (pickle) | 💥 | 💎 | 💥 | 💎 | 💎 | 💎 | 💥 |

Although often thought of as synonymous with Native American pieces, turquoise has a long history in other types of jewelry as well. Because the color of turquoise was symbolic for "forget me not," it was used in many sentimental pieces during the Victorian era. Turquoise has seen a recent resurgence in popularity, with many sophisticated designs featuring the stone in yellow and white metals.

Mined in many areas around the world, turquoise is found in association with copper, from which it gets its blue to green color. The American Southwest has plentiful sources for turquoise, which often has an appearance that is specific to its mine. Mine names such as Sleeping Beauty, Bisbee, and Kingman can evoke a specific color and texture in the mind of a turquoise connoisseur. Other sources around the world include China, Mexico, Chile, and Iran. Iranian turquoise is the fabled Persian turquoise that has an even, bright blue color and takes a very high polish.

Turquoise is a somewhat porous stone with a variable hardness depending upon its source and exact chemical makeup. The

harder or more dense the turquoise, the higher the polish the stone will take. This is why some turquoise appears to have a waxy luster when polished, while other stones are very lustrous. Turquoise also may have veining or matrix present. An inclusion of the host rock that is trapped in the turquoise, matrix can be nearly any color, with the most common being brown, white, or black. Turquoise with attractive patterns of black matrix is often referred to as "Spider Web" (Figure 1).

## Enhancements and Imitations

Turquoise is often, if not almost always, enhanced. Most enhancements are geared toward stabilizing the color of the stone. Due to its porosity, turquoise absorbs many substances that it encounters during daily wear. Skin oils, lotions, mineral-rich tap water, and soap are just a few of the substances that can be absorbed by turquoise and change its color. A stone that was purchased in a robin's egg blue color can turn green or darken from the absorption of various common substances over a few months of wear. To stabilize the color, turquoise is treated with a wide range of substances to reduce its porosity. On the low-tech end of the enhancement spectrum are simple procedures, such as rubbing the stone with melted candle wax or paraffin. Other, more advanced methods include applying resins such as Opticon, which is designed to seal fractures and fill pits in gemstones.

The color of turquoise can also be enhanced through the use of dyes, which turquoise will absorb easily, thanks to its porosity. Treatments can also satisfy the desire for certain veining patterns; for example, black matrix can be imitated simply by applying black shoe polish or paint to uneven surfaces.

Another turquoise treatment is the "Zachery Process." This proprietary process results in an even, stable color with high luster.

# Quick Tips

### Rock Solid Facts
- Mohs Hardness: 5 to 6
- Cleavage/Fracture: Conchoidal or granular

### Tools That Rule
- A laser welder for repairs with the stone in place.
- A lid for the pickle pot to avoid accidental pickling.
- Metal polishing compounds designed specifically for green turquoise.

### Bench Check
- Have you avoided pickle, which can dull and damage coatings and backings?
- Have you used polishing compounds designed specifically for turquoise?
- Are the seats in your turquoise-set piece cut properly to avoid stone breakage?
- Have you removed the stone before performing any torch work?

### Design Check
- Can the turquoise in your design be removed if a repair is necessary in the future?
- Have you used malleable metals and multiple thin prongs in your design to reduce the pressure needed during stone setting?

### Features and Benefits
- Turquoise is affordable for any budget.
- Turquoise is often used in dramatic designs that would be extremely costly if made with other gems.
- Turquoise is recognized as one of the December birthstones.

The process uses turquoise's porosity to absorb a substance that actually *decreases* the porosity, creating a smoother surface, higher polish, and a stabilized color.

Turquoise treatments are sometimes easily identified. Black matrix added to the stone becomes apparent when viewed microscopically. Some coatings are also visible using a microscope, or will sweat when exposed to a heat source. Other treatments can't be easily identified. The Zachery Process is nearly undetectable and is best addressed by a gemological laboratory. However, definitive identification of a turquoise treatment is often a very low priority because the cost of testing is often greater than the cost of the stone. Many turquoise dealers claim to be able to instinctively tell if a stone has been enhanced. However, when colleagues of ours tested the "experts" against sophisticated chemical analysis, the human instinct for turquoise treatment was shown to be a miserable failure.

Another issue with turquoise is that it is often backed with epoxy to add strength to a stone. This is done by coating a side of a turquoise piece with a thick layer of any kind of epoxy-type substance. This can be done before or after the stone is shaped and polished, and the treatment is visibly obvious. The exception is if a stone is set in a closed-back setting that covers the epoxy.

When dealing with turquoise, it is safest to assume treatment if you aren't sure.

You can also find imitation and synthetic turquoise on the market. Common imitators include dyed blue howlite, although it is usually very dull and has a too-bright blue color. Synthetic (laboratory-produced) turquoise is made in plain blue and with matrix. It has a very even tone and will take a high polish. Microscopic examination by a gemologist will reveal structural characteristics that separate synthetic from natural turquoise.

Other turquoise-inspired products are reconstituted turquoise, plastic, and chip inlay. The most common version of reconstituted turquoise is ground turquoise reformed with binders and other compounds into a solid material. Plastic is self-explanatory, and chip inlay consists of small chips of turquoise suspended in clear epoxy.

## Clean It

The inherent porosity of turquoise makes cleaning problematic. Do not place turquoise in an ultrasonic because the cleaning fluid can soak into the stone and cause a color change. The cleaner may also remove common wax-based treatments used to stabilize the color, again producing a color change. The epoxy backings on turquoise can also sustain damage from an ultrasonic. Steam cleaning can have the same effect.

## Picture This

> This stone shows the porous nature of turquoise. Note the waxy polish and somewhat "gritty" appearance of the surface.

< This stone has been polished with normal metal polishing compounds. At left is the stone before polishing and at right is the stone afterward. The black compound accumulated in the stone's cavities and could not be removed with a brush and soap or with ultrasonic cleaning.

> These two stones used to match until the stone on the right was subjected to a torch flame (approximately 10 seconds of exposure). The stone changed color and sintered (pieces are missing from the surface).

< While the stone on the right is undamaged, the stone on the left was subjected to indirect heat from a torch. This resulted in the black staining that is not removable.

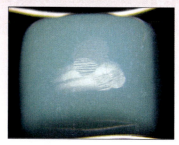

> This stone illustrates the softness of turquoise. The deeper grooves are the result of one light pass with a file. The finer-textured dull area is the result of a single pass with a sanding stick. This relatively high polish turquoise will have to be repolished.

Another potential problem in cleaning is that turquoise often is set in silver with oxidized patterns (or has been painted black to resemble oxidation). Steam or ultrasonic cleaning can easily damage the oxidation or the black paint. This can result in having to do a time-consuming oxidation or repainting job on an often very inexpensive piece.

It is best to clean turquoise with warm water, preferably distilled, to prevent any color changes in the stone.

## At The Bench

Turquoise must be handled with the utmost care at the bench. Avoid any contact with chemicals or polishing compounds, which can be absorbed into the stone's surface and cause color changes. Buffing compounds can leave black smudges on the surface that are very difficult to remove. For green turquoise, use metal polishing compounds designed specifically for that stone (Figure 2).

Do not pickle turquoise-set pieces because pickle can dull the stone and damage coatings and backings. To avoid accidentally pickling a turquoise piece, keep the cover on your pickle pot.

Turquoise and heat do not mix—in fact, the stone can actually explode when exposed to a torch. To complicate this problem, a great deal of turquoise is set in silver, which conducts heat very effectively. This makes any type of torch work extremely risky, even if a heat shield or water bath is used to protect the stone. Therefore, remove the turquoise before doing any torch work. (Lasers are a good alternative for gold and platinum.) Even though much of the turquoise on the market is not overly expensive to replace, each stone has a unique appearance, and it can be time consuming to match a broken stone.

Because turquoise is somewhat soft, it can break easily when pressure is applied during the setting process. Added to this is the tendency of some turquoise stones to have backs that are not flat. Therefore, be sure to cut all seats to fit a stone's profile (including an uneven back) to avoid added pressure during the setting process. In addition, if a setting features thick, hard prongs, take care to cut the seats correctly so as not to create pressure points.

## Design It

When designing turquoise jewelry, choose metal alloys that are more malleable, such as platinum or 18k yellow gold, because they require less pressure to bend over the turquoise, thus reducing the chance of damage. Also, use multiple small prongs instead of a few heavy prongs to lessen the pressure needed to bend the prongs over the stone.

## Care for Wear

Turquoise, even if stabilized, may change color with long-term daily wear. To help maintain a stone's color, your customers should avoid lotions, soaps, and other absorbable substances while wearing turquoise. Activities as commonplace as doing dishes can and probably will affect the color of the stone. Wearers who work out and perspire on their turquoise will notice color changes, as will those who are avid swimmers or hot tub users. In short, wear your turquoise but keep it out of any substance that can be absorbed by the stone.

Turquoise will also lose its polish if worn regularly in a ring or bracelet. To restore the stone's luster, recommend that customers bring in their stones for repolishing.

# Gemstone Resources

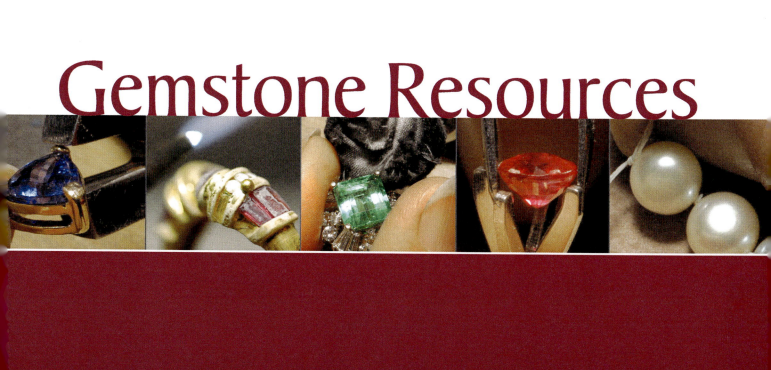

# Resource Index

117    Diamond Council of America

118    GCAL (Gem Certification & Appraisal Lab)

119    GIA (Gemological Institute of America)

120    National Association of Jewelry Appraisers (NAJA)

121    Neutec/USA

122    Otto Frei

123    Rio Grande

## GEMSTONE RESOURCES

# Diamond Council of America Addresses Changes in Industry

The recent and dramatic changes in the jewelry industry have changed the way many jewelers do business. Issues such as shifts in sources and supply channels, the production and availability of synthetics, political and social concerns surrounding conflict diamonds, the move toward branding, in tandem with the increasing number of online diamond retailers have transformed the business.

Retail jewelers have been hit hardest by these rapid shifts. Key to maintaining and growing their business is the success of their sales staff.

In response to the demand for educational tools that can address the changing climate in the diamond and jewelry industry, Diamond Council of America (DCA) launched its updated and revised Diamond Course in September of 2021. "It is so important to stay in step with industry trends," says Terry Chandler, President of the DCA. "In an environment that seems to be in a constant state of flux, the DCA Diamond Course provides training on topics that are new, but important to our industry."

The DCA's original Diamond Course provided members and their staff with comprehensive training in diamonds. The distance learning program educates sales staff on topics key to developing strong sales skills. Topics covered in the program include cut, grade, and the mine to the store process.

Additions to the Diamond Course include topics such as presenting branded diamonds, as well as updated information regarding synthetics, treatments, and simulants, including details about disclosure.

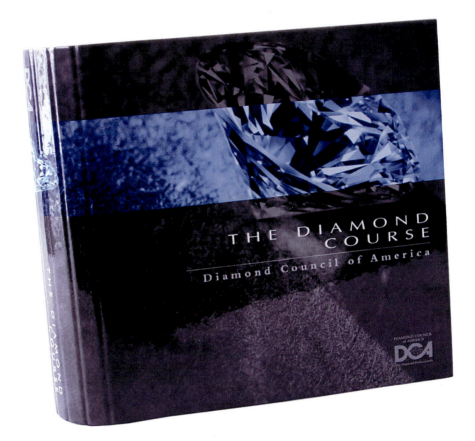

The revised diamond course also offers expanded sections regarding client development (with an action plan for associates to implement) and the latest tools and techniques to promote your store and utilize sales measurements.

"The DCA believes education and training are a jeweler's best defense in this economy," says Chandler. "Our revised Diamond Course gives our members the edge they need to grow their businesses."

For more information about DCA and their educational programs visit their Web site at *www.dcalearning.org* or call: 877-283-5669.

**DIAMOND COUNCIL of AMERICA**

The Diamond Professionals

**Diamond Council of America**
3212 West End Avenue, Suite 202
Nashville, TN 37203
1-877-283-5669 or
1-615-385-5301
Fax: 615-385-4955
*www.diamondcouncil.org*

# GCAL by Sarine: A Better Customer Experience for Both Natural and Lab Grown

### THE WORLD'S HIGHEST STANDARD

GCAL developed the 8X Ultimate Cut Grade to recognize the best of the best diamonds. Today, over 70% of all natural round brilliant diamonds and over 85% of lab-grown diamonds are given "excellent" cut grades. Less than 1% of those qualify as 8X by being graded "excellent" on eight factors: polish, external symmetry, proportions, optical brilliance, fire, scintillation, optical symmetry, and hearts and arrows (shape aesthetics on Fancies).

### ADD VALUE TO YOUR DIAMOND INVENTORY

Diamonds that qualify as an 8X are noticeably brighter and more brilliant than ordinary "excellent" cut grade diamonds. "Once my customers see an 8X, they can't buy anything else," says Cub Root of Form to Feeling in Austin, Texas. "It makes it a whole lot easier to sell diamonds." Every 8X Cert demonstrates to your customers why your diamonds are better, and includes an exceptional quality 360° video and stunning Fire video.

### PREMIUM LAB GROWN

The 8X Ultimate Cut Grade is available for lab-grown diamonds too, giving you the opportunity to differentiate your lab-grown inventory from the competition and offer your customers an affordable way to own the best of the best.

### GUARANTEED GRADES

GCAL is the world's only gem lab that guarantees its grades in writing. This money-backed grading accuracy guarantee elevates the GCAL diamond document from report to certificate and gives your customers total confidence. Each 8X diamond has the 8X logo inscribed on its girdle for extra security.

### BUY SIGHT UNSEEN

When a diamond meets the tight 8X parameters, you instantly know it meets the highest cut standard. In fact, the 8X Ultimate Cut Grade is so precise that you can confidently order the world's most brilliant and beautiful diamonds for your customers, even sight unseen.

### PRINCESS PERFECT

The 8X Ultimate Cut Grade is also available for princess-cut diamonds, giving you the opportunity to trade up your customers who love this modern silhouette to a premium cut with proportions and craftsmanship that guarantee superior light performance and near perfect symmetry.

### GOODBYE BOW TIE

Why should customers who love the elegance of oval, pear, and marquise diamonds settle for less brilliance and beauty than they deserve? The 8X Ultimate Cut Grade is available for oval, pear, and marquise shaped diamonds too. You can be confident these 8X diamonds minimize the bow tie effect and are beautifully cut, every time.

### THE FUTURE OF DIAMOND GRADING

GCAL analyzed hundreds of thousands of diamonds to create each 8X shape, basing the standards on data and direct assessment of the light performance of diamonds that passed through the GCAL lab. And now GCAL is backed by global diamond technology leader Sarine, innovating diamond certification with AI-powered eGrading and built-in traceability. Together GCAL and Sarine are creating the future of diamond grading.

GCAL BY SARINE
1-212-869-8985
sales@gcalusa.com
GCALUSA.com

# Advance Your Bench Skills With Gem Expertise from GIA®

For over 90 years, GIA has been at the forefront of gemological expertise, with an unwavering mission to protect consumers and ensure the public trust in gems and jewelry. GIA created the 4Cs of diamond quality, launched the first gemology education course in the U.S., and patented the first gemological microscope and jeweler's loupe. From gemology to bench jewelry, to 3D modelling and design, GIA is committed to sharing gemological knowledge at every stage of a jewelry professional's journey.

## GIA Graduate Jeweler Diploma Program

Offered only at the GIA World Headquarters in Carlsbad, California, the GIA Graduate Jeweler diploma program prepares students for successful careers in jewelry fabrication and repair. Graduate Jeweler students work hands-on with gemstones and precious metals using professional-quality tools at individual workstations.

Studying under the guidance of experienced instructors, students acquire strong foundational gemstone setting skills and practice setting a wide variety of cuts, such as round, trilliant, emerald, baguette, princess cuts, and more. Throughout this 26-week program, instructors demonstrate optimal methods for stone setting to ensure the protection of gemstones throughout the jewelry manufacturing process.

At GIA's ocean view campus in Carlsbad, Graduate Jeweler students are immersed in gems and jewelry through numerous educational gem and jewelry displays throughout the campus, enjoy access to the Richard T. Liddicoat Library, home of the world's largest collection of gemological and jewelry-related books and periodicals, and can embark on exciting tours and trips to local gem mines.
**Learn more at *GIA.edu/GJ*.**

## GIA Graduate Gemologist® Diploma Program

A Graduate Gemologist diploma from GIA is the hallmark of a highly trained jewelry professional. Through both deep theoretical knowledge and extensive hands-on practical work, students learn to identify and evaluate diamonds and colored gemstones using specialized gemological equipment under the direction of experienced GIA instructors. This includes understanding how gemstone hardness, durability, cleavage, and other factors affect setting and cleaning. This program imparts confidence in buying, selling, evaluating, and working hands-on with gemstones.

This widely recognized credential can be earned at GIA campuses in Carlsbad and New York as well at other GIA campuses worldwide or through GIA Online

Education combined with in-person lab classes. **Learn More at *GIA.edu/GG*.**

Each GIA campus is located in a gem or jewelry hub, helping students enrich their knowledge of the industry both on and off campus. Broaden your career horizon, expand your network, and deepen your skillset with a credential from GIA today.
**Explore More at *GIA.edu/education*.**

GIA's Carlsbad campus is accredited by the Accrediting Commission of Career Schools and Colleges (ACCSC).

©2024 Gemological Institute of America, Inc. (GIA). All trademarks are registered trademarks owned by GIA. GIA is a nonprofit 501(c)(3) organization. All rights reserved.

**GIA World Headquarters
The Robert Mouawad Campas
5345 Armada Drive
Carlsbad, CA 92008
1-800-421-7250
or 1-760-603-4000
*www.GIA.edu***

## GEMSTONE RESOURCES

# The National Association of Jewelry Appraisers

## Serving the Professional Jewelry Appraiser with Pride©

### Who We Are

In the past 40 years, a number of appraisal organizations have established protocols that have taken the appraisal profession to new heights. We at The National Association of Jewelry Appraisers (NAJA) are proud to have been one of those organizations. We are the largest appraisal organization devoted solely to the appraisal of gems and jewelry. Our members (now more than 700) sign on to observe a stringent Code of Ethics and we also request that they appraise to the Report Writing Standards (RWS). We constantly try to make them aware of legal problems which may be encountered by doing otherwise. The RWS is taught in the Appraisal Standards Course (ASC) and constantly updated so that they and their clients are protected with a properly researched valuation for the particular purpose needed. We feel we have made NAJA the place to achieve the knowledge necessary to make gem and jewelry appraisers true professionals and help keep them updated on the latest techniques, equipment, and information within our constantly changing industry.

### It's All about Education

We do this through the online ASC, quarterly *The Jewelry Appraiser* newsletter, and discounts on books and equipment, as well as by serving as a sounding board for questions concerning our profession. The ASC also teaches sections of the government-sponsored Uniform Standard of Appraisal Practice as it relates to the appraisal of personal property. In addition, we hold two conferences each year with diverse speakers who are experts in their fields and offer timely topics and information to help update the knowledge needed. At these conferences our members have the chance to network with their peers and find colleagues with whom they can share information and experiences.

### Our Other Benefits

NAJA's website addresses the needs of the consumer as well as members of the jewelry industry with the "Find an Appraiser" function. Our appraisers are listed by city, state, and specialty for people who need an appraiser. We also answer questions from the public and the trade to help them understand what an appraiser can offer. We have served to help unravel problems between the appraiser and the client.

Today, the appraisal profession is a necessary part of the jewelry industry and we take great pride in the fact that we are a strong part of it.

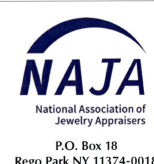

National Association of Jewelry Appraisers

P.O. Box 18
Rego Park NY 11374-0018
1-718-896-1536
*www.NAJAappraisers.com*

## GEMSTONE RESOURCES

# From Vision to Creation

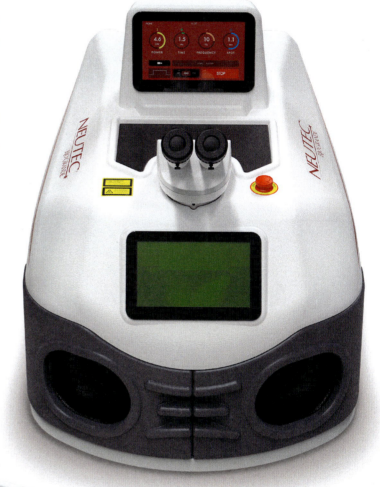

Upgrade your soldering station with a Neutec® PulsePoint™ Studio™ Plus 220 laser welder and dial in on precise connections. Affordable, lightweight and compact, this machine offers high-duty, professional technology without taking up precious space in your studio. With a built in Leica® microscope, large weld chamber and high-efficiency optics, the Neutec Plus 220 is a jewelry-manufacturing benchmark.

Visit *riogrande.com* and search "laser welder" to learn more.

### Specifications:
- Laser crystal: Nd-YAG 7mm bar
- Wavelength: 1064nm
- Maximum pulse power and duration: 25mS at 220 joules
- Peak pulse power: 9kW
- Average power: 90W
- Spot diameter: 0.1-2mm
- Voltage: 115-230 volts (single phase)
- Frequency: 50/60Hz
- Dimensions: 20" x 29.25" x 22.25"H

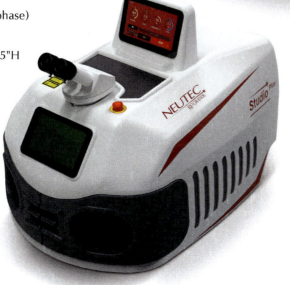

**RIO GRANDE®**
Since 1944

Rio Grande
7500 Bluewater NW
Albuquerque, NM 87121
1-800-545-6566
Fax: 800-965-2329
*info@riogrande.com*
*www.riogrande.com*

## GEMSTONE RESOURCES

# For Superior Stone Setting
## Otto Frei Lets You Do Your Best Work

Where does quality jewelry start? Some would say it's in the selection of the best metals. Others might suggest that it's all a function of a well-thought-out design. Still others might offer that quality stems from the work process itself. Ask Steven Frei, president of Otto Frei in Oakland, California, and he'll tell you that quality starts with the bench you work on—and the best benches in the jewelry business come from Otto Frei.

"The John Frei Custom Work Bench is the best quality bench jewelers can buy," Frei says. "When we first came out with this bench 40 years ago, we weren't sure we could sell it because it was, and still is, more expensive than other benches. But we found that jewelers were thrilled to have a bench of this quality.

"Some of the largest jewelry manufacturing shops in the United States have outfitted their jewelers with our benches," Frei adds. "They want to show their jewelers that they're appreciated, so they give them the best workstations."

The John Frei Custom Work Bench is built in cabinet-quality solid maple or oak with a 2-inch-thick butcher-block top, and it comes fully assembled. The standard bench is 49 inches wide—almost a foot wider than most other commercially available benches. Choose from six different stock models or have the company create a custom bench to suit your needs. Whatever size, shape, wood, color, or options you want, Otto Frei can make it for you. When a customer doing remount work recently needed a bench on wheels, he got it from Otto Frei.

Once you've treated yourself to the best bench, you'll want to be sure it's equipped with the best tools—and you'll find them all with Otto Frei. "We're known for carrying the highest-quality tools and equipment from top manufacturers around the world," Frei says. "And we're always on the lookout for more." Recent additions include Otto Frei's Setter's Microscope, as well as new disc mass-finishing systems.

"Although we offer all the classic hand-finishing tools and the best polishing buffs and compounds, these disc finishers are saving jewelers a lot of labor," Frei says. "You can get hand-polishing-quality results in under an hour."

Otto Frei is also the place to go for your platinum jewelry needs, offering the best in platinumsmithing tools, including the widest selection of platinum polishing products on the market. "We have products from Germany, Japan, Italy, and the United States," Frei says. "People have their preferences, and we let them decide what they want."

If there's one thing everyone wants, it's quality, and that's why so many jewelers turn to Otto Frei. From the products on the bench right down to the bench itself, if you want to do your best work, work with Otto Frei.

**119 Third Street**
**Oakland, CA 94607**
**1-800-772-3456**
**or 1-510-832-0355**
*ottofrei.com*

## GEMSTONE RESOURCES

# Source, Polish & Protect Your Gemstones with Rio Grande

### Protect Yourself
Accurately identify loose and mounted gemstones with the Yehuda Sherlock Holmes 4.0 and protect yourself against fraud. This gemstone tester recognizes natural and synthetic diamonds in the D–K color range, moissanite, CZ and CZ coated with synthetic diamond. A long (internal) UV test checks fluorescence in diamonds and has a 100% detection rate. The Yehuda is ready to use in less than a minute, delivering color-coded results that can easily be uploaded to your Google drive or other cloud account.

### Limitless Design Possibilities
Rising in popularity, radiant lab-grown rubies, sapphires and emeralds are chemically and physically identical to their natural counterparts. Explore an incredible selection of stunning hues, shapes and sizes that offer your customers expansive options.

### Cabochon Polishing Perfection
Tested and recommended by Swiss professionals, the new AGILO® CABSHINE easily remove scuffs and scratches from your cabochons. They're safe for use on hard and soft gemstones using only a rotary tool and light pressure—no water required—without unsetting the gemstone and risking damage to your mounting.

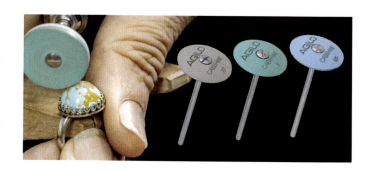

### Safe & Easy Jewelry Cleaning
Gentle enough for everyday use, the Clean + Care® jewelry cleaning kit comes with everything you need to keep your jewelry sparkling like new. The cleansing formula effectively removes dirt, oil and grime without rinsing or agitation. Complete with a basket, brush and layered polishing cloth, this kit comes in attractive packaging that is perfect for gifts and add-on sales.

Since 1944

Rio Grande
7500 Bluewater NW
Albuquerque, NM 87121
1-800-545-6566
Fax: 800-965-2329
*info@riogrande.com*
*www.riogrande.com*

# About the Authors

**Arthur Anton Skuratowicz, GJG, CGA,** is a third-generation jeweler who developed his skills in his family's Chicago area store. After studying communications and drafting in college, Arthur attended the Gemological Institute of America (GIA), where he completed the Graduate Gemologist and Graduate Jeweler programs. Following his completion of GIA courses, Arthur became the first instructor hired to teach both gemology and manufacturing arts at GIA. A Certified Gemologist Appraiser, Arthur then went on to serve as a sales associate, jeweler, and appraiser at an American Gem Society retail firm.

**Julie Nash, GJG, ASA, Master Gemologist Appraiser®,** grew up on a Registered Hereford cattle ranch in the isolated high country of Colorado and became a silversmith during her senior year of high school. While attending college, Julie continued crafting silver and gemstone jewelry, and her creations were featured in Saks Fifth Avenue in Paolo Alto, California. After earning a B.A. in Studio Art at Colorado College, Julie attended GIA, where she completed the Graduate Gemologist and Graduate Jeweler programs. Soon after she completed the requirements of the American Society of Appraisers to become an Accredited Senior Appraiser and Master Gemologist Appraiser®.

After marrying in 1995, Arthur and Julie left their teaching positions at GIA and relocated to Albuquerque, New Mexico, to get back into jewelry retail. In 1999 they moved to Colorado Springs, Colorado, where they started Anton Nash LLC Appraisers. Arthur taught design at GIA New York and later started The Jewelry Training Center in Colorado Springs for jewelry trade professionals and hobbyists. Although they since have amicably split as a couple, they remain close confidants; Arthur now works as a bench jeweler in the Chicago area while Julie continues Anton Nash LLC Appraisers.

Made in the USA
Las Vegas, NV
11 December 2024

13774754R00076